JIHAD

The Mahdi Rebellion In The Sudan

JIHAD

The Mahdi Rebellion In The Sudan

Second Edition

BY

MURRAY S. FRADIN

Authors Choice Press

New York   Lincoln   Shanghai

Jihad
The Mahdi Rebellion in the Sudan

Authors Choice Press
an imprint of iUniverse, Inc.

For information address:
iUniverse
2021 Pine Lake Road, Suite 100
Lincoln, NE 68512
www.iuniverse.com

Second Edition

ISBN: 0-595-27881-7 (Pbk)
ISBN: 0-595-74749-3 (Cloth)

Printed in the United States of America

Dedicated

to

The Memory

of

My Mother

ACKNOWLEDGEMENTS

The manuscript of this book has been read by Professor Oscar I. Janowsky of the City University of New York. His observations, comments, and suggestions have proved of value in many instances and I wish to express my appreciation of them. I also wish to acknowledge the aid which Professor Louis L. Snyder gave me regarding technical matters. I wish to express my thanks to the War Office and Public Record Office in London whose prompt replies to my inquiries regarding the locations of Mahdist source materials facilitated the completion of my research. I am indebted to Mr. Richard Hill and Professor Peter M. Holt of the University of London, School of Oriental Studies for advising me on the locations of specific Mahdist documents. Finally, I want to thank Mr. Malik of the Government Archives, Ministry of the Interior, Government of the Sudan for sending me a detailed list on the locations of specific Mahdist materials.

Responsibility for views and opinions expressed in this book is, of course, my own.

Update to Recent Events

This book is going to press just as the United States is completing a mass offensive in Iraq, toppling the Saddam Hussein Regime, and setting the stage for a post-war government.

In this context, *JIHAD: The Mahdi Rebellion in the Sudan* presents, in the author's view, a totally overlooked dynamic in the Middle East and one that needs to be addressed—the force of militant Islam. This force represents a rallying point for hundreds of millions in the region.

When I first drafted *JIHAD*, it was written as the history of a nineteenth century religious war in an isolated portion of the world—the Sudan. This war, led by Mohammed Ahmed, a self-proclaimed Moslem prophet and military leader, was directed against the ruling governments in that region, the British, the Egyptians, and, even, the Turks. At one point, this charismatic Moslem leader even had visions of sweeping across West Africa and threatening French interests there. A vast fundamentalist movement called Mahdism had begun to emerge.

Today, we are witnessing a similar phenomenon. Radical Islamic forces are moving into positions of power all over the Middle East. They are capturing the minds and hearts of millions of people in that region.

Moreover, several European nations including Great Britain and France, with much more experience in the Middle East than the United States, have warned that a war in Iraq coupled with a post-war occupation will further inflame the entire region and bring back visions of Western imperialism.

It is the firm belief among the majority of the people of the Middle East that the key element driving the current military-political situation is purely economic—that is, based on the politics of oil.

With the rise and development of new inventions and new technologies, millions of people throughout the Middle East, and indeed, the world have begun to move into the ranks of the middle class. This higher standard of living has, inevitably, created sharp demands for energy—translated to oil. The Middle East being the main repository of this high-ly-prized natural resource, the spectre of a resurgence of Western imperialism seems all but inevitable to the average Arab.

Just as the Mahdi Mohammed Ahmed raised a vast army in the Sudan of 1881 in a move against the British and their allies, so Fundamentalists today are inciting their forces against the West. We may be faced with a new type of war-fare and confrontation—JIHAD!

It is up to America, together with rational minds in Europe, the Middle East, Asia, and North Africa to set an agenda by which the Islamic and Western Worlds can live in mutual peace and respect. There is too much at stake and time is running out.

It is with this vision that I have chosen to bring out this new edition of *JIHAD: The Mahdi Rebellion in the Sudan*. It is a wake-up call and MUST reading for every intelligent person who wishes to understand the total dynamics of the Middle East, why this region may be on the verge of explosion, and how such a disaster may, possibly, be averted.

Murray S. Fradin
New York City
May 2003

JIHAD
The Mahdi Rebellion In The Sudan 1881-1885
TABLE OF CONTENTS

Chapter 3
The Religious Causes

Geographic, cultural, and economic aspects of Sudanese Islam — Precepts of the Koran — Eschatological elements of Sudanese religion — The manifestation of the Mahdi Mohammed Ahmed — Mahdism as a result of political factors — Visions of a resurrection in Upper and Lower Egypt — The 'Hijra' and the 'Jihad' — 'Ansar' and 'Jihadiya' — The Mahdi Mohammed's power over the tribes of Darfur, Northern and Central Kordofan, and the Red Sea Hills — Asceticism of the Mahdi and his followers — Bracing for the struggle

Chapter 4
Political and Military Synthesis: The Sword of Islam

British attempts to consolidate control in the Sudan — The struggle in Westminster: Gladstone, Baring, Malet, Granville — Gordon succeeds Sir Samuel Baker in the Equatorial Provinces — Romolo Gessi, Rudolf Slatin, Emin Pasha, Chaillé-Long, and Father Joseph Ohrwalder — The Mahdi's 'Ansar' and the 'Khalifa' system of command — Osman Digna's Beja warriors in the Mahdia — The capture of El Obeid — Battles of Shaykan and Tamaii — Khalifa

Abdullahi and the Emirs — Ansar advance on Khartoum — Siege and capture of the city

Chapter 5
General Gordon and the Sudan:
A Brief Biographical Sketch

Chaillé-Long's evaluation of Gordon's character — 'Chinese' Gordon's experiences in the Crimean War and Taiping Rebellion — Gordon's appointment to the Equatorial Provinces — Gordon's abhorrence of slavery — Gessi's defeat of Suleiman's forces in the Bahr el-Ghazal — Gordon and Zubeir Pasha: allegations and counter-allegations — The Mahdist uprising of 1881 and Gordon's recall to the Sudan — The siege and fall of Khartoum

PREFACE

In 1881 the Sudan witnessed a political and religious movement of paramount importance not only for the Arab world but for all of Europe as well. The Mahdi Rebellion ushered in a period of struggle against colonialism. It thwarted for a period of almost twenty years England's imperialist ambitions in the Sudan. The purpose of this book is to examine the underlying causes of the Mahdist movement, and to trace its early development up to 1885.

In the course of my book, I am including the Khedival period in Egypt which begins in 1863 with the reign of Khedive Ismail. I hope to relate the Mahdist outbreak in the Sudan with the depreciating economic situation in Khedival Egypt. This study will also attempt to show the effect of Egyptian misrule and taxation on the political and religious turbulence in the Sudan. I refer here to the so-called "Bashi-Bazouks" who became both feared and hated for their excesses in the collection of taxes from the populace.[1]

With the outbreak of hostilities in 1881, the Mahdist revolt entered its military stage. Therefore, from 1881 to 1885 I shall be dealing, to a large extent, with the political-military picture as it affected both England and the Sudan, and also with the debates and decrees of Parliament,

[1] This was the name given to the tax officials who administered a corrupt taxation agency in the Sudan. Many of these 'Bashi-Bazouks' were recruited from the ranks of the Shaiqiya tribe, a group which inhabited territory south of the confluence of the Atbara and the Nile.

i

government communiques to the renowned General Gordon, and policy statements by members of the House of Commons, including the prime minister, Gladstone.

A special section is devoted to the religious causes of the revolt. This will deal principally with the Mahdi's interpretation of the Koran and, specifically, with the peculiar eschatological elements of Sudanese Mohammedanism. Sudanese Islam will be viewed in the context of the political conditions of that time. I have been fortunate to obtain original materials in this area including the diary of Father Ohrwalder,[2] the memoirs of Rudolf Slatin,[3] the accounts of Chaillé-Long,[4] and the official proclamations of the Mahdi, himself.[5]

In this same section, the Mahdi Mohammed Ahmed undergoes some careful scrutiny. His personal appearance, character, education, and religious outlook are examined in the light of contemporary descriptions by such authorities as Slatin Pasha and Father Joseph Ohrwalder.

[2.] Wingate, F. R., Ten Years' Captivity in the Mahdi's Camp, 1882-1892: From the original manuscripts of Father Joseph Ohrwalder. (London, 1892)

[3.] Slatin, R. C., Fire and Sword in the Sudan (London, 1896)

[4.] Chaillé-Long, C., The Three Prophets: Chinese Gordon, Mohammed Ahmed (El Mahdi), Arabi Pasha. Events before and after the bombardment of Alexandria. (New York, 1886)

[5.] The official proclamations of the Mahdi are included in the British Sessional Papers, volume 88, 1884. They are listed under 'Correspondence respecting the Affairs of Egypt.' These parliamentary papers are available in micro-printed form in the Economics Division of the New York Public Library.

The influence of General Charles George Gordon upon the Sudan will be examined in some detail. I have written of Gordon only in so far as he relates to the Sudan picture during the Mahdist outbreak. There are some references to his previous life in Equatoria, and in China, but these are incidental to his main role of Governor-General of the Sudan immediately prior to the revolt, and as military commander of the garrison at Khartoum during the siege of the city in 1884-1885.

The last section is concerned with the historical analysis of the Mahdist revolt. It recapitulates the main causes of the rebellion and raises such questions as: What is the legacy for the Middle East of this movement? Can such mysticism ever foster another "Mahdi" outbreak? Are the Sanusi movements of the present-day a key to Mahdism?

Finally, the conclusion is reached that the Mahdi Rebellion in the Sudan was not simply a local religious upheaval. It was the final and violent expression of a people who had found a leader with whom they could identify their despair at economic and political oppression at the hands of the corrupt Egyptian regime. In this sense, then, the Mahdi's cause was the last active ingredient added to an already volatile political and economic mixture.

MURRAY S. FRADIN

CHAPTER

1

Introduction

The subject of the Mahdi revolt has undergone
many romantic interpretations. General Gordon is
depicted as the British knight-errant in a barbarous and uncivilized land while the Mahdi is
described as a religious prophet following a grand
destiny. Though there are elements in this period
which lend themselves to a romantic and dramatic
historical narrative, the objective here will be a
sober historical analysis.

Much has been written on the military course of
the Mahdi Rebellion but not very much on the
underlying causes. I have grouped the causes into
three basic categories: religious, political-
economic, and military-cultural. The last
category represents the union of a warrior-
oriented tribe with the cause of Mahdism. These
tribes include the Baggara, Hadendowa, and the
Arabic-speaking groups of central and northern
Kordofan.

James, in his book, The Wild Tribes of the
Sudan,[1] described the nature and character of

some of these tribes from personal field experience, notably the Basé people who occupied, at that time, a small area of land between Tokar and Abyssinia:

> The Basé are the bêtes noires, moreover, of all that part of the Sudan, and have the character of being a very treacherous and unfriendly people; so that it was not only on the part of the Egyptian officials that we expected to have obstacles thrown in our way, but we felt sure that we should have considerable difficulty in getting camel-drivers and servants to undertake the journey. Then, too, the Basé, dwelling as they do between Egyptian and Abyssinian territory, ...might think that, instead of being bent purely on travel and sport, we were really come on behalf of the Egyptian Government to endeavor to squeeze taxes out of them, and to reduce them to submission. [2]

In his book of travels James described the caravan and trade routes from Egypt to the Sudan and their importance to Europe's transport of merchandise from Sudan's port cities. He wrote:

> The great caravan route from Suakin is that which, crossing the desert, strikes the Nile at Berber, a distance of two hundred and forty miles; not the road to Cassala, which we followed. Its trade...is not increasing, owing ...to the restrictions on the slave-trade. Formerly, slaves could be purchased with

cotton-cloth imported from Manchester; and
the slaves were made to carry ivory, ostrich-
feathers, etcetera, to the coast; now this
'branch of industry' is done away with, although
more merchandise finds its way to Europe by
Suakin than by the other great outlet, that via
Berber and Korosko on the Nile. [3]

In another section, he discussed the similarities in physique and general appearance between
the nomadic Sudanese Arabs and the ancient
Egyptians. James said:

No traveler in these parts can fail to be struck
by the great similarity in physique and general
appearance of many of the wandering tribes
of Arabs, to the ancient Egyptians as depicted
on the walls of their temples and tombs. The
mode of wearing the hair is identical; the
curious little wooden pillows they use for
their heads when sleeping are exactly of the
same form and make as those which may be
seen in museums containing ancient Egyptian
curiosities... [4]

Indeed, the Sudanese tribesman incorporated
the unique blend of Egyptian and Central African.
He was dark in color, and possessed pronounced
Semitic features. Yet, despite the similarity of
physical characteristics, tribal and cultural divisions kept him apart from his neighbors in the
northern Sudan. It was not until the Mahdist
rebellion that a pronounced change occurred.
Mekki Abbas has written:

The ethnographical and tribal divisions of the
northern and central Sudan were, for the first
time in modern history, weakened by the
Mahdist revolution against the corrupt Turko-
Egyptian rule. The revolution had a religious
basis and the various tribes that rallied behind
the banner of the Mahdi did so as fellow
Moslems united in their jihad [5] by a common
cause... [6]

Though the Sudanese people have a certain
resemblance to the Egyptians, and though their
language contains similarities to Egyptian fellah
Arabic, their cultures and folk spirit were
different.   In this way, the Sudanese tribes
retained an individual cultural core and heritage.
According to Abbas:

The Egyptian claim that present day Egyptians
and Sudanese are racially and culturally one
and the same people can only be partially
justified.   The vast majority of the northern
and central Sudanese are, like the majority
of Egyptians, Moslem in religion and culture.
There is also, in varying degrees, common
Caucasian and Arab blood.   Nevertheless,
there are differences between the populations
of Egypt and the northern and central Sudan
which make it difficult, if not impossible, to
regard them as being as homogeneous and
as assimilated as the people of any unified
modern state.   As regards language, the
Arabic spoken by the Kababish of northern
Kordofan or the Baggara of Darfur or the

Shukrin of Cassala is no nearer to Egyptian
fellah Arabic than that of Morocco or Hadra-
mout. The usage and the intonation are
different, and so is the folk lore. [7]

The differences between the Sudanese and the
other Arabic groups of the Middle East, at this
time, were the result of geographical barriers.
Whereas Egypt lay on the Eastern Mediterranean,
the Sudan was situated well inland, away from any
large body of water except for the border with the
Red Sea. Much of the land was desert or semi-
desert and except for the construction of very
basic communications facilities by British outposts and military bases at the end of the nineteenth century, the general picture of the territory
was one of primitive development.
The Nubians, as the ancient Sudanese were
called, were a blend of many peoples, and their
progeny perpetuated this mixture of different
ethnic groups. Abbas said:

The whole physical and social environment is
unlike that of Egypt. These differences are due
to geographical and ethnic barriers. The bulk
of the Arabs of the Sudan were until the
improvement of the means of communication
in the twentieth century, cut off from the
Arabic-speaking people of Egypt by the desert
and by the Nubian tribes who live along the
Nile between Aswan and Dongola, a distance
of no less than 500 miles...The average
Egyptian is nearer to the Mediterranean
types...whereas the ordinary Sudanese is

nearer to the African. Dr. Taha Hussein goes
as far as saying in his Future of Culture in
Egypt [8]   that the Egyptians are by culture
and outlook more Mediterranean and European
than Oriental and Islamic.   The ordinary
Sudanese knew no influence from the Mediterranean... [9]

The discontent that reared its head in this dry
and sandy place and culminated in the Mahdi revolt
can be traced even further back than 1881. Egypt
had always been of great importance to England's
colonial position for she lay astride the Suez
Canal, England's main communications line to
her African and Asian possessions. England and
France both had vital interests in Egypt and the
Suez Canal Zone. According to A. J. P. Taylor,
Egypt was

> vital to both countries—vital to the British
> government for reasons of imperial strategy,
> vital to the French because of tradition and
> prestige.   The Egyptian question had been
> created by Bonaparte when he led his ex-
> pedition there in 1798.   The British had
> answered by expelling him without establishing
> themselves. [10]

On the influence of the Suez Canal Taylor had
this to say:

> ...the geography of world-power was revo-
> lutionized by the Suez Canal, Napoleon III's
> most lasting memorial.   Though the British

had steadily opposed the Canal for obvious strategical reasons, they became the principal users of it as soon as it was open; in 1882, 80 per cent of the ships passing through the Canal were British. Here was a stake in Egypt which it was impossible to repudiate, a stake increased when Disraeli acquired the Khedive's shares in the Canal in 1875. [11]

The Dual Control in Egypt by the British-French combination coupled with a depreciating Egyptian economy led to popular unrest. There was particular resentment among the Sudanese people against the corrupt officials, and especially the notorious "Bashi-Bazouks". James, in his travel accounts, said:

By far the worst soldiers in the Sudan are undoubtedly the irregulars (Bashi-Bazouks); and I can fully endorse the opinion of Lieutenant-Colonel Stewart in his report on the Sudan recently presented to Parliament... (Stewart) says, 'They are a constant menace to public tranquility. As soldiers, they are valueless, having no discipline...' [12]

Unrest soon grew into political-military action and a nationalistic spirit was born. The Egyptian soldiers, motivated by a sense of patriotism, and coupled with hatred for both the European and Turk, rose against the government. Led by one of their senior officers, Colonel Ahmed Arabi, they forced the resignation of the Minister of War in January, 1881. They were soon joined by

other nationalist groups, and together they succeeded in dismissing the entire ministry in
September of the same year. In January, 1882,
British and French government officials presented
the Egyptian government with the Gambetta Note
[13] which stated that both governments regarded
the maintenance of the powers of the Khedive as
axiomatic to the preservation of law and order in
Egypt. The refusal of the Arabi government to
yield on these points, and its attempt to force a
nationalist ministry upon the Khedive prompted
England to send warships into the harbor at
Alexandria and demand the immediate resignation
of the Arabi regime. Europeans domiciled in the
city were also given assurances by England that
their rights would be protected. To further com-
plicate matters, the other powers of Europe,
including Germany, Italy, and Russia, issued notes
attesting their desire to see the status quo
maintained in Egypt.

Rioting broke out in Alexandria in 1882 with
the resultant slaughter of scores of Europeans
by surging mobs of Arabs. When one of Arabi's
coastal batteries fired upon the English warships,
the naval bombardment of the city began. In a
short while, all the Egyptian guns were stilled
and English forces began landing operations
along the Mediterranean coast.

While the English were beginning their occupation operations in Egypt in 1882, not very
much attention was paid to events in the Sudan.
Yet it was there among the primitive and religious
peoples that England was to face her greatest
threat to Middle East security. The man behind

the budding anti-European movement was Mohammed Ahmed, a native of Dongola. As a youth,
Ahmed spent a great part of his time studying
the Koran and the teachings of the Sudanese
sheikhs. He developed an ascetic outlook on life,
renouncing all luxuries and comforts. After his
initiation into the deeper mysteries of Islam,
he went to live on Abba Island in the Nile.
Sartorius' personal travel narrative of the Sudan
of 1885 described the early development of
Ahmed's thought and actions. [14]

> When Ahmed was about twelve years old, he
> went up to Khartoum to join his uncle. While
> there he...attached himself to the following
> of a sheikh. These sheikhs are a peculiar
> institution in the Sudan; they are supposed to
> be men under the special protection of a
> particular angel of God, whose interposition
> is effected by the sheikh having isolated
> himself for eight or nine hours daily during
> a term of years...constantly repeating all
> that time one of the ninety-nine names of
> God...the individual in question (then) declares
> himself invested with the power of the angel...
> takes the name and dignity of sheikh, collects
> a following of dervishes round him, and pro-
> ceeds to live upon the offerings of other
> people. It was in this way that Ahmed went
> on. [15]

In accordance with his convictions that the
truly pious Moslem should wear only scanty,
unpretentious clothing, he lived on Abba Island

in the White Nile dressed in the most scanty and
dirty clothes.   Here, in a cave, he spent many
hours each day muttering the name of Allah, and
in every way acting the role of a great religious
zealot.   At last, in the year 1881, he emerged
from his cave and announced to his followers,
who were daily increasing, that he was the
expected Mahdi.   Coincidentally, this announcement came at the time that Arabi's rebellion in
Egypt was entering its final death throes.

By the end of 1882, the Mahdi had assembled
a large, ill-equipped force of his Ansar [16]   and
proceeded to march on Bara and El Obeid in
Kordofan.   Fired with a religious fervor, they
took both cities with little loss. It is significant
to note that these cities were garrisoned by large
Egyptian forces, well-armed and in possession of
great stores of ammunition. Despite this formidable resistance, the Mahdi's forces pursued the
offensive with such determination that all were
swept from their path of advance.   Sartorius
pointed out:

> ...it is not...astonishing that the prestige of
> the Mahdi increased to such an extent that his
> every word was considered sacred. How could
> it be otherwise, when all his followers were
> not even armed with spears and swords, but
> many had only sticks, and yet found themselves
> without loss, and in possession of all these, to
> them, wonderful things...[17]

One of the most authoritative accounts of the
Sudan situation at this time and an excellent study

of personalities was Colonel Chaillé-Long's The
Three Prophets 18 which revolves around the
personalities of Gordon, the Mahdi, and Arabi
Pasha.   Chaillé-Long was an officer in the
Egyptian Army, and first met Gordon when the
latter appointed him chief-of-staff to his military
command in the Equatorial Province of Africa.
Of the Mahdi, Chaillé-Long wrote:

> The Mahdi, during the author's service in
> Africa, was living in obscurity in Khartoum,
> or in his hermitage on the White Nile. He
> was associated, there is but little doubt, with
> his Dongola people, in the slave and ivory
> hunting, the common occupation of the Dongo-
> lowee.   Mohammed Ahmed has since pro-
> claimed himself a prophet and has been sancti-
> fied by the faithful as Mahdime, the sub-
> lime. 19

Arabi was a lieutenant-colonel in the Fourth
Regiment when Chaille-Long was serving on the
General Staff of the Egyptian Army.   He met
Arabi during the rebellion which began in Alexandria in 1882.   Chaillé-Long said that Arabi
Pasha and Mohammed Ahmed sought the same
ends, Arab unification in the face of European
political and military power. They differed only
in their methods: Arabi fought under the banner
of political reform; the Mahdi fought under the
banner of Islam.
    Gordon was both catalyst and dynamic agent
in this potpourri of religious, political, and
military activity.   Finally, in 1885, the forces of

Islam in the Sudan, led by the Mahdi, besieged the garrison at Khartoum.   It was here that General Charles George Gordon fought his Armageddon against overwhelming forces.   A sea of pent-up emotion, aroused by years of oppression and misery was let loose upon this lone bastion of Anglo-Egyptian authority.   A storm was raised that would take twenty years to abate.

CHAPTER

2

The Political and Economic Background

When those states which have been acquired are
accustomed to live at liberty under their own
laws, there are three ways of holding them. The
first is to despoil them; the second is to go and
live there in person; the third is to allow them
to live under their own laws, taking tribute of
them, and creating within the country a government composed of a few who will keep it friendly
to you.

— from Machiavelli's <u>The Prince</u>

CHAPTER

2

The Political and Economic Background

Chaillé-Long said: "When Ismail Pasha ascended the throne of Egypt in 1863, his fortune was insignificant. When he left it he had become the proprietor of immense domains." [1]

Corruption was rife in Egypt at this time and it was apparent that the government treasury was being depleted in an unscrupulous manner. The Commissioner of the Debt, upon taking charge of the finances, soon discovered that great sums of revenue were being diverted from the treasury. The Minister of Finance admitted that he had applied these revenues to the "urgent needs of the Khedive." [2] The Khedive handled the situation in typically oriental fashion. Fearing that a closer examination of Egypt's finances by England might prove embarrassing and create a scandal, he had his finance minister, Ismail Sadyk Pasha, arrested on charges of inciting a revolt against the Khedive. On the 15th of November, 1876, the following announcement was made in Cairo:

The ex-Minister of Finance, Ismail Sadyk
Pasha, has sought to organize a plot against
His Highness the Khedive by exciting the
religious sentiments of the native population
against the scheme proposed by Messrs.
Goschen and Joubert. He has also accused the
Khedive of selling Egypt to the Christians, and
taken the attitude of defender of the religion of
the country. These facts, revealed by the
inspectors-general of the provinces, and by the
reports of the police have been confirmed by
passages in a letter addressed to the Khedive
himself by Sadyk Pasha...In presence of acts of
such gravity, His Highness the Khedive caused
the matter to be judged by his privy council,
which condemned Ismail Sadyk to exile, and
close confinement at Dongola. [3]

On the 4th of December, Ismail Sadyk's death
was announced. There were, however, suspicions
about his death. Rumor had it that years before,
the Khedive had arranged a railway accident at
Kaffir Azyayat that was meant to shorten his road
to the throne by the death of Ahmed and Halim.
According to Chaillé-Long's account:

The princely party were returning from Alexandria to Cairo. Said Pasha, the Viceroy, had
given a great fête in the former city. Prince
Ismail should also have been there, but he made
illness his excuse and was absent. As the train
bearing its royal freight came thundering along
to the river, too late the engineer saw before
him the open draw and the deep raging Nile

below. The train went into the river, one car upon the other, with a frightful crash. Halim Pasha, skilled in athletic sports and with great presence of mind, leaped from the carriage into the river and swam ashore. Ahmed was a fat, ponderous man—he could not follow, and was lost. The murder of the Mouffetish, Ismail Sadyk, brought vividly to remembrance and apparent confirmation the suspicions which attached to Ismail in procuring the death of Ahmed. [4]

When Khedive Ismail attempted in April, 1879 to terminate the Dual Control in Egypt, England and France, together with the other European powers brought pressure to bear on the sultan, who, on the 26th of June, deposed Ismail, and replaced him by his eldest son, Tewfik. The economic state of Egypt at the time can best be summed up by the special report made by Mr. Cave on the financial condition of Egypt:

The critical state of the finances of Egypt is due to the combination of two opposite causes. Egypt may be said to be in a transition state, and she suffers from the defects of the system out of which she is passing, as well as from those of the system into which she is attempting to enter. She suffers from the ignorance, dishonesty, waste, and extravagances of the East such as have brought her Suzerain (Ottoman Empire) to the verge of ruin, and at the same time from the vast expense caused by hasty and inconsiderate endeavors to adopt the civilization of the West.

Immense sums are expended on unproductive
works after the manner of the East, and on
productive works carried out in the wrong way,
or too soon. (This last is a fault which Egypt
shares with other new countries for she may be
considered a new country in this respect, a
fault which has seriously embarrassed both the
United States and Canada; but probably nothing
in Egypt has ever approached the profligate
expenditure which characterized the com-
mencement of the Railway system in England.)...
The Khedive has evidently attempted to carry
out with a limited revenue in the course of a
few years works which ought to be spread over
a far longer period, and which would tax the
resources of much richer exchequers. [5]

The Khedive's accounts were kept in a careless
manner, (not following any consistent plan or
pattern). The situation was described by Mr. Cave:

That the accounts are kept in a slovenly,
imperfect manner is evident on the face of
them. Take for instance the Budget for 1876,
and the *Compte Rendu* for 1875, which contain
items jumbled together in a most extraordinary
way, such as a railway in the Sudan and a canal
in Egypt in one sum. If we examine the
accounts of the Customs, which are under the
Finance Minister, we shall find no complete
official table of the imports and exports of each
Custom-house in Egypt, specifying the kind, the
quantity, the value, and place from whence they

came, or their destination. Moreover, the returns of quantity are made on no principle whatever, being sometimes according to weight, sometimes according to number, size of parcel, so many pairs, etcetera. [6]

The history of Egypt and the Sudan is tied directly to the history of imperial England. This is made clear in the writings of Sir Reginald Wingate, one of the great developers of the Anglo-Egyptian Sudan. In the edited works of Sir Reginald Wingate by Sir Ronald Wingate, the latter points out the relationship between Egypt, the Sudan, and England. In the era of Khedive Ismail, that is, Egypt from 1863 to 1879, England tried to consolidate her commercial position in the Middle East. [7]

It has been said that England acquired her Empire in a fit of absence of mind. This sweeping statement, if not altogether true, is correct to the extent that the Empire was not the result of an imperial dream, of an ideal, or of rapacity. It was the result, for the most part, of individual effort with little or no support from the Government of the day; and of perfectly sensible and obvious decisions taken at different times to meet the political, military or economic necessities of the moment. One commitment produced another, one acquisition necessitated further expansion. The case of England and Egypt was, however, quite different. Here, no military, political, or economic, far less imperialistic—to use the term in its worst sense—considerations played any part. [8]

Wingate said that a series of circumstances arose in Egypt which were not correctly evaluated in both France and England.   This incorrect evaluation resulted, firstly, in precipitate action with respect to commerce, and then, in military measures.   England and France had not taken account of political, economic, and military factors in Egypt in their zeal for commercial advantages.

The English soon found themselves in the role of a military occupation force in Egypt in 1882

...without any clear conception as to why they had got there, but with the uneasy feeling that they should not be there, with the determination to get out as quickly as possible, but with no idea at all as to how this praiseworthy intention was to be implemented. [9]

The economic situation of Egypt, the corruption in high government places, the nationalist stirrings in the Egyptian Army among the followers of Arabi, the presence of European dignitaries and their families domiciled in Cairo and Alexandria, created the anti-foreign feeling that was to lead simultaneously to the riots in Alexandria and the Mahdist revolt in the Sudan.   The Egyptian crisis revolved around political, economic, and military factors; the Sudanese outbreak had its main impetus from the spiritual leadership of the Mahdi. The defeat of Egyptian field forces by the Mahdi's army during 1881-1885 can partly be traced to the demoralization of Egypt's military forces by inner political and economic corruption. The men that the British led in their expeditions against the Dervishes were not imbued with a sense of nationalism nor were they filled with any form of selflessness or fanaticism   in support of a righteous cause.   They were simply military levies, raised by the British to quell what seemed to England at first, an audacious but minor rebellion in Upper Egypt. They were swept away like so many pawns by the growing army of the Mahdi.

To understand the development of Egyptian nationalism and Sudanese Mahdism we must go back to 1863 in the reign of Ismail Pasha. The political and economic circumstances of that period sowed the seeds of political and military revolution in Egypt and religious-military revolt in the Sudan. When Ismail Pasha came to the throne of Egypt in 1863, he found himself in control of a large country with plentiful natural resources, and a prosperous economy caused by the American Civil War. When southern ports in the United States were blockaded by Union forces, Egyptian cotton achieved new levels of trade on the continent. Egypt developed her railroads, canals, and shipping docks, and the Suez Canal was in the process of completion. Cairo and Alexandria, the two great transit points for trade on the Nile and in the Mediterranean, respectively, were populated by European settlers. Communications

improvements had been introduced from Europe,
and Egypt seemed to be approaching a modern
political state industrially and economically.
However, political rule in Egypt was still oriental
in nature; the ruler had many absolute powers that
included both political and fiscal matters. In
economic matters, Egypt's national picture fell on
the debit side of the balance sheet. According to
Wingate, the debit side had three main items:

> ...the first, a public or Khedival debt computed
> in 1876 at 91 million pounds; the second, a
> system of administration and an administrative
> personnel that was inefficient; the third, a
> commitment in the Sudan which was onerous
> both militarily and financially. All these three
> items were interconnected, but it was the first,
> without much regard to the second and with no
> regard at all to the third, which engaged the
> attention of Europe, and particularly of England
> and France. [10]

The Khedival debt arose because of a series of
loans advanced by the merchant banking houses of
England and France [11] over an eleven year
period, beginning in 1862. These loans were made
to meet the deficits in current Egyptian revenue. [12]
England and France, the two countries chiefly
concerned with Egypt's economy, sought to secure
a regulation of Egyptian finances. The situation
was summed up succinctly by Wingate:

> In the first place England and France supported
> the full demands of the foreign creditors; in the

second place they used their influence with the
ruler of Egypt to secure—and this must be
frankly stated—the priority of these demands
over the requirements of Egypt and its responsibilities as regards the Sudan. In the
third place, while looking upon Egypt as a
bankrupt estate to be administered in the
interests of the creditors, they left the management of the estate in the hands of the owner
who had brought about the situation, and hoped
by giving him a small staff of what were
virtually European accountants, to influence
him to reform his management. The duty of
these accountants was to tell the Khedive that
of every pound that came into his treasury,
more than ten shillings should be paid to his
foreign creditors. [13]

England had political and strategic interests in
Egypt besides her strictly economic and commercial interests. This was brought out clearly
in a government policy statement:

The leading aim of our policy in Egypt is the
maintenance of the neutrality of that country,
that is to say, the maintenance of such a state
of things that no great Power shall be more
powerful there than England. [14]

The statement went on to say that English
presence in Egypt together with the introduction
of English capital would involve political and
military responsibilities that would go far beyond
mere financial speculation. Egypt, on the contra-

ry, said the statement, should endeavor to establish native rule within the limits of liberal
but efficient government administration. If England could not maintain a liberal regime in Egypt,
and some barbarous administration came to
power, then some other great power might be
tempted to intervene in her affairs. In another
part of the statement, the English point out that
the creditors of Europe, including Austria,
France, Germany, and Italy, might decide to take
an active interest in Egyptian affairs, even to the
point of political and military intervention. [15]
This would go against English interests. Above
all, England maintained a dominant interest in the
coastal areas of Egypt bordering on the Eastern
Mediterranean. Her policy was made very clear
in the official statement:

> It should...be borne in mind that if the Ottoman
> Empire were to fall to pieces, and Egypt
> became independent, the part of Egypt which
> interests England is the sea-coast, including
> the railway and other communications across
> the Isthmus. If it should happen that Egypt
> were divided, and the sea-coast and communi-
> cations remained under the dominant influence
> of England, while the interior were to be
> otherwise disposed of—supposing the stability
> of such an arrangement could be guaranteed—
> England would have no reason to be dis-
> satisfied with it.
> In the disposal, therefore, of European ap-
> pointments, it is of primary importance to
> keep in English hands, as far as may be

possible, the harbors, customs, light-houses, and the communications by land and water from sea to sea.   It is only of course to a limited extent that this can be done; and the necessity is not sufficiently urgent at present to justify steps which would awaken the jealousy of other Powers.   But the extension and consolidation of English influence upon these points is the object which, as regards the future, must be kept in view.   Whether it shall be pursued slowly or energetically must depend upon the circumstances of the moment.[16]

On the 8th of January, 1882, the governments of England and France submitted a special note to the Khedive of Egypt intended to restore effective government in Egypt.   It became known as the Gambetta Note, after its author, Leon Gambetta, the French Foreign Minister at the time.   It was issued in response to Arabi Pasha's demonstration before the viceroyal palace on September 9th, 1881 which led to Khedive Tewfik's acceptance of a representative government together with a larger army.   The main points of the Gambetta Note include the following excerpts:

You have already been instructed on several occasions to inform the Khedive and his Government of the determination of England and France to afford them support against the difficulties of various kinds which might inter-fere with the course of public affairs in Egypt.

The two Powers are entirely agreed on this
subject, and recent circumstances, especially
the meeting of the Chamber of Notables
convoked by the Khedive, have given them the
opportunity for a further exchange of views.
I have accordingly to instruct you to declare
to the Khedive that the English and French
Governments consider the maintenance of His
Highness on the throne, on the terms laid down
by the Sultan's Firman, and officially recognized by the two Governments, as alone able to
guarantee, for the present and future, the good
order and the development of general prosperity in Egypt in which France and Great Britain
are equally interested. [17]

When England and France issued their col-
lective decree to the Khedive, there was a sharp
protest from the Sublime Porte. It was in the
form of an official note to the British Foreign
Secretary, dated January 13, 1882. It said in
essence that British and French moves toward
Egypt, though they were made ostensibly in the
name of justice and equal treatment, were suspect.
The Sublime Porte phrased his case thus:

In view of the Imperial Firman which the
Sublime Porte has promulgated relative to this
province, and the proceedings of the recent
Turkish Special Mission, the step taken by the
two Consulates-General shows that the re-
iterated assurances of the Imperial Government have not been appreciated. We cannot,
therefore, disguise the painful impression

which it has made upon us, and we find
ourselves compelled to submit some observations upon it to the sentiments of justice and
equity of the English Government.

Always to protect the immunities granted to
Egypt, and thus to preserve the order and
prosperity of this province, is the sincere wish
and interest of the Imperial Government,
whose efforts up till now have been directed
towards this end...Nothing...justifies the col-
lective communication which has just been
made to His Highness Tewfik Pasha, especially
since Egypt forms an integral part of the
possessions of His Imperial Majesty the Sultan,
and since the power conferred upon the Khedive
for the maintenance...of order and public
security, and...proper administration...comes
...within the rights and prerogatives of the
Sublime Porte.[18]

On February 2, 1882, Foreign Secretary
Granville received a communiqué from the British
Ambassador at Istanbul regarding the views of the
other Powers, specifically, Russia, Italy, Austria,
and Germany, on the matter of the Sublime Porte's
reply to the Gambetta Note. The Powers declared
that they wished a status quo to exist in Egypt.[19]

The important point to remember is that the
liberal Gladstone administration, though it purported to represent a just and equitable settlement
for Egypt, and the establishment of a strong
Egyptian government consistent with the aims of
English interests in the Middle East, it had
already assumed direct political responsibility

when it established the Dual Control.   The
Gambetta Note was simply another, and clearer,
example of this direct political interest in Egypt's
internal affairs.   As a result of the Gambetta
Note and the Sultan's reply to it, British policy
moved more and more toward direct opposition
to the Arabi forces in Egypt.

Arabi, in the meantime, had not been idle.   In
1876, he had formed a secret society among the
fellah officers. Five years later, on January 17,
1881, Arabi and his [20]   seven officers met at
Abdin and drafted a *pronunciamiento* in which
the fellah officers protested special privileges
accorded the Circassian, Turkish, and foreign
officers in the Egyptian service. He followed this
move by forcing the resignation of the Minister of
War, one Osman Rifki, and installing in his place,
Mahmoud Sami El Baroudi, an Arabi supporter.

In September, 1881, another *pronunciamiento*
was made at Abdin. This time, Arabi demanded
a constitution and a larger army from the Khedive.
The Arabi clique grew more adamant in their
demands. When the Khedive asked them what they
wanted, they replied: "Accord us our demands or
we have your successor in readiness." [21]

The new ministry under Arabi underwent a
good deal of satirical comment in the journals of
the time.   One journal described the path to
advancement under the Arabi regime through the
case of three particular aspirants:

'Do you not remember that it was I who pulled
Rivers Wilson's beard three years ago?'

'Ah, it is true,' replied Arabi. 'You pulled
Wilson's beard; tiib, you shall be made a
major.'

'You exclude me from advancement, but I am
the one who was the first to enter the palace
of Abdin in February.'

'Pardon, I had forgotten; you shall be a
colonel.'

'How is this you leave me without promotion?
I deserted my post when I was on guard at the
Ministry of War, when you should have been
tried by the court-martial, and when your
troops delivered you.'

'You are right. For this service you deserve
to be named a general.' [22]

What the Mahdi Mohammed Ahmed, the Dongo-
lowee, had done in Upper Egypt to gather sup-
porters to his cause of a great jihad, Arabi Pasha
began doing in Lower Egypt—donning the cloak of a
great religious figure.   Unfortunately, the cloak of
a great religious fanatic did not fit easily over the
military uniform of the young Egyptian colonel.
Though Arabi did succeed in luring followers to
his nationalistic banner, he never achieved the
fanatical and devotional homage accorded the
Mahdi.   Arabi, according to Chaillé-Long, was
directly responsible for the brutal massacres of
Europeans in Alexandria commencing in June,
1882. On the night of June 10th, he said, a secret
council was held in Cairo at which were present
Arabi, Toulba, Ali Fehmy, Nedim, Said Khandil,
the Prefect of Police of Alexandria, Suleiman
Daoud, and Hassan Moussa-el-Akhad. The object

of this meeting was to preach against the "foreigners" and prepare for the brutal beating of the
foreign populace of Alexandria.   Chaillé-Long
said:

> Moussa-el-Akhad and Nedim left Cairo by the
> train for Alexandria on Sunday morning of the
> 11th.   They arrived there shortly after midday.
> At three o'clock, at a given signal in the Rue
> des Soeurs, the fiendish work began.   The
> time was well chosen.   Sunday afternoon—the
> ...Place des Consuls was filled with the élite
> of Alexandria.   Toward this place rolled the
> tide of Arabs, armed with *naboots*, a stout
> stick...which had been distributed...by the
> police.   They fell upon the...populace...brutally
> beat them down... [23]

Word of this outbreak of direct violence
against Europeans domiciled in   Alexandria
reached all the great Powers.   England was
especially concerned with the situation as it
involved an imminent threat to her Eastern
Mediterranean communications.   In an official
communiqué to Earl Granville, Sir Edward Malet
briefly outlined the situation as it then stood:

> My Lord: With reference to my dispatch of the
> 19th ultimo, I have the honor to enclose,
> herewith, copy of a further and final report
> which I have received from Mr. Keith Grosjean,
> detailing additional evidence which he has been
> able to procure respecting the massacres of
> the 11th June.   In closing his report, Mr.

Grosjean expresses his regret that many broken links in the chain of evidence still exist, and states his opinion that to correct them a Juge d'Instruction with the fullest powers would be required. I have, etcetera. [24]

Mr. Grosjean's communiqué to Edward Malet included some interesting evidence of an organized plan of massacre and brutality against the *nosorani* —European Christians. In his report, he made clear that the weapons used— *naboots* in this case—were distributed by the police at the edge of the European quarter. At a given signal, the Arab mobs were directed against the throng of Europeans gathered at the Place des Consuls. A few brief excerpts will suffice to illustrate the chain of events that led up to the massacre.

Sir: Confirming my previous report of the 10th ultimo, and in pursuance of your instructions to close the same, I have the honor to report as follows:

With regard to the distribution of naboots I have obtained evidence that on the afternoon of the 11th June last, one Ahmed-el-Gouda, a dealer in Naboots, carrying on business at Wacha Mow, Sikket-el-Ghedidah, near the Fort Napoleon, distributed large quantities of naboots to the mob...at about 3 P.M. persons showing themselves at the windows, or on the terraces of their houses were fired at...

I have information that a signal for the rising was given to wit, a feigned funeral of an Arab

followed by persons, probably sheikhs, several
of whom wore green turbans, passing on the
morning of the 11th June last, the day of the
massacre, through the main and minor streets
of Alexandria...feigned, because such funeral
procession coming from the lower quarter of
the town had...if...real...no reason...to pass by
the European quarter...
I submit that the above facts all tend to show a
preconcerted scheme... [25]

Admiral Seymour, commander of Her Majesty's fleet outside the harbor of Alexandria ac-
knowledged receipt of an emergency message
from the British Minister at Cairo:

Viceroy says if men land from the ships, or
the garrison apprehend hostile action, there
will be a general conflagration throughout the
country. The representatives of the powers
are now going to Dervish Pasha to attempt to
obtain a temporary arrangement by which the
security of the Christians may be insured... [26]

In Alexandria, the European consulates issued
a joint proclamation to the foreign citizens of the
city. It was posted in the form of a public
placard and read:

Fellow citizens: Grave disorders have broken
out in Alexandria. The Egyptian army and its
chiefs engage themselves to re-establish order
and cause it to be respected. We have con-

fidence in it.   We are in perfect accord with the civil and military authorities upon the measures necessary to assure public tranquility.   We appeal to your wisdom to aid us in the accomplishment of this common task... [27]

Arabi's ministry began construction on the shore defenses surrounding the harbor at Alexandria and strengthened the shore gun batteries at Ras-el-Tin and the southern shore of the harbor. On the 6th of July, Admiral Seymour sent the following communiqué to Toulba, the Egyptian officer in charge of the shore defenses:

I have to notify your excellency that unless such proceedings be discontinued, or if, having been discontinued, they should be renewed, it will become my duty to open fire on the works in course of construction. [28]

When the Egyptians refused to dismantle their guns, Admiral Seymour initiated a naval bombardment of the city.   The firing began early in the morning and lasted until noon when the three British naval vessels, Sultan, Superb, and Alexandria were joined by the Inflexible, and directed the final fire which silenced the remaining guns in the forts at Ras-el-Tin and the fort at Adu.   The naval bombardment of Alexandria initiated the British occupation of the city and the thrust into Upper Egypt.

Up to this point, the sole interest of England and the other European Powers was to maintain the status quo of Lower Egypt and, especially, the

Eastern Mediterranean zone. Now, a new threat reared its head from the sands of Upper Egypt; British interests in Egypt seemed to be under threat of attack from this southern quarter by the ever-growing forces of the Mahdi. Yet, despite this obvious danger to British garrisons in the Sudan, there was an equal danger to the security of the Mahdi's own forces from the neighboring kingdom of Abyssinia. In 1876 at Kaya Khor, King John of Abyssinia with an army of one-hundred thousand men,   defeated the Egyptian Army, capturing a great deal of war material.   The Mahdi Mohammed Ahmed made overtures to King John with the purpose of forming an alliance between the evolving Mahdist state and the state of Abyssinia. King John's reply was short and to the point:

The letter of Johannes, King of the kings of Ethiopia to him who is Prophet with the Turks

...Thou hast written me. I am a great prophet. I do not wish to dispute with thee. Let there be peace between us.
I do not know if the will of God is that we may go to war...but what does that signify? Is it not in our hearts? I am a Christian and thou art a Mussulman. There, where I am, thou canst not be; there, where thou art, I cannot live in peace.[29]

It was for reasons of security, then, that the Mahdi hesitated to move his forces down the Nile into Lower Egypt. Had he done so early in his career, he would have left a formidable Abyssinian force on his flanks.

Sir Samuel Baker spoke harshly on the Sudan question.   He advised that England must not abandon the Sudan, that "England must be mistress of Egypt.   To evacuate the Sudan would be an indelible dishonor." [30]

Chaillé-Long pointed out that the abandonment of the Sudan was in direct violation of the rights of the Sultan of Turkey. The Firman of investiture given to Khedive Tewfik on August 17th, 1879 included the following clause:

> The Khedive shall not, under any pretext or motive, abandon to others, in whole or in part, the privileges accorded to Egypt, and which are emanations of the rights and natural prerogatives of my imperial government, nor shall he abandon any part of the territory. [31]

The Gladstone administration found itself in a trying situation on the matter of British policy toward Egypt and the Sudan. Controversial positions were held in the British Parliament. The Sudan, especially, became a thorn in its side. Though "abandonment of the Sudan pacified the Radicals, it antagonized the Forward wing of the Liberal party." [32]

In the parliamentary debates of 1883-1884, the Conservatives censured the British government's Sudan policy. The Times and the Pall Mall Gazette, leading British journals of the time, bitterly criticized abandonment of the Sudan on the grounds that it represented an act of "shirking the

imperial mission of civilization.'' [33]   Further,
Egypt and the Sudan were passageways to India,
England's greatest dominion.   Any abandonment
of this territory would mean the severing of her
communications with the East. The queen stated
her country's policy succinctly:

> ...it is of absolute necessity to secure to
> ourselves such a position (short of annexation)
> in Egypt as to secure our Indian Dominions
> and to maintain our superiority in the East. [34]

The Sudan represented a peculiar problem to
England. On one hand, England did not wish to
plant its foot overtly in the Sudan; on the other
hand, she wanted to maintain order and stability
there.   It fell on her, then, to support the establishment of Egyptian outposts in the area. On
Egyptian government in the Sudan, however,
England's leaders took a dim view; Egypt was not
ready nor able to govern such a large territory.
According to MacMichael:

> The British Government declined even to take
> any part in the choice of officers to be
> recruited for staff duties in the Sudan. The
> only proposal that received accent was to send
> a British officer, not 'in any military capacity',
> but solely to report on the situation. The
> choice fell upon D.H. Stewart. He proceeded
> south at once, and his report was published
> early in 1883. His main recommendation was
> in a passage which stated:
> 'I am firmly convinced that the Egyptians are

quite unfit in every way to undertake such a
trust as the government of so vast a country
with a view to its welfare, and that both for
their own sake and that of the people they try
to rule, it would be advisable to abandon large
portions of it.' [35]

Stewart advised the British government that
Egypt should limit her activities to the northern
Sudan, and to the area east of the White Nile.
Equatoria and the rest of the country he advised
to be left to the rule of the sheikhs and former
rulers.

Stewart, a keen observer, also concluded that
the Mahdi revolt was local in nature, limited to
the region around the provinces of Kordofan for a
period of two years. If the revolt had been a truly
political and national one, Stewart reported, the
Mahdia would have immediately spread throughout
the Sudan. As it was, even when the Mahdi had
taken Khartoum in 1885, the Mahdia never reached
the northernmost areas bordering on Lower Egypt
nor the borders of Equatoria in the south.

Holt contends that the Mahdi Mohammed Ahmed achieved such great political, military, and
religious power in the Sudan because of the
power-vacuum left when Khedive Ismail was
deposed in 1879, and a puppet ruler, Tewfik, put
in his place by the Great Powers of Europe. This
state of events carried away the last remnant
of prestige in Egyptian royalty.

Another factor in the rise of Mahdism was
General Charles George Gordon. Gordon was sent

to the Sudan during and after the reign of Khedive Ismail to make an estimate of the situation and then put things in order. He captured the imagination of many of the inhabitants of the Sudan. Gordon got along well with Ismail and both men saw eye to eye on the important issues facing Egypt and England in the Sudan. When Ismail was deposed and Gordon left the Sudan temporarily, a power-vacuum resulted. It was to be filled by a fanatical Sudanese Moslem: Mohammed Ahmed of Dongola.

CHAPTER

3

The Religious Causes

The burden of the desert of the sea. As whirl-
winds in the desert pass through; so it cometh
from the desert, from a terrible land.

— Isaiah

We swear allegiance to God, His Prophet, and to
you, by God's unity, that we will not associate
anything with Him, nor steal, nor commit adultery,
nor accuse anyone falsely, nor disobey you in
rightful things. We swear that we will renounce
this world, being content with what God has
decreed, desiring God's mercies in this world
and the next, and that we will not flee from the
jihad.

— The Mahdi's Bai'a Oath from Shouquair, iii,
    page 139.

CHAPTER

3

The Religious Causes

The Mahdi Mohammed Ahmed arose out of a combination of local circumstances, not the least of which were the power-vacuums left by Ismail and Gordon. With no effective civil or military authority in the Sudan, the Mahdi's power grew to gigantic proportions by 1885. Under his disciple, the Khalifa Abdullahi, the Mahdist state was extended even further. Right up until 1898, when General Herbert Kitchener administered a decisive defeat upon the Khalifa's force at Omdurman, Mahdist power reigned supreme in the Central Sudan.

To understand the power which the Mahdi wielded over his followers,[1] it is necessary to fully understand the geographical, economic, cultural, and religious factors in the lives of the Sudanese. Trimingham has written a thorough account of Sudanese Mohammedanism[2] in which he brings together all of these factors. The

Sudan is a large country containing about a million
square miles. It is bounded by Egypt on the north;
by the Red Sea, Eritrea, and Abyssinia on the east;
by Uganda and the Belgian Congo in the south; and
by French Equatorial Africa on the west. The only
natural boundaries of the Sudan are the Abyssinian
Hills in the east and the Nile-Congo watershed
in the west. Trimingham said:

> To understand the life-apprehensions of the
> Sudanese then we have to take into account two
> movements: one due to the life-process of the
> people in contact with their geographical
> environment: while the other, Islam, is one
> which is a universal church and a cultural and
> social system common to a number of different
> peoples and resulting from intellectual and
> religious interaction and synthesis. Only by
> taking both these movements into account is it
> possible to understand these people. [3]

The most important geographical feature in the
Sudan is the Nile with its tributaries. The White
Nile enters the Sudan through rapids; then it
continues to flow through the swamps of the
sudd, [4] emerging into the bush country between
Malakal and Kosti, and finally joining with the
Blue Nile at Khartoum. At the same time, the
Nile gathers the waters of the Upper Nile,
Bahr-el-Ghazal, Bahr-az-Zarafa, and the Subat
to create a regular annual supply of water for
irrigation and small-scale farming.

Transportation into the interior region at this
time was usually by two chief means, the Nile and

the desert caravan. Much of the land is desert, devoid of vegetation. With the exception of the vast plains along the Nile River banks, the rest of the country is unsuitable for urban dwelling. Between the coast and the Nile lies the Nubian Desert, on the west, part of the Libyan Desert and the Bayuda Desert. The Red Sea Hills mark the eastern flank of the great Rift Valley. South of the desert is shrub steppe, "typical nomad country which produces abundant pasturage for camels and goats at certain times of the year owing to a regular if scanty rainfall."[5]

The peninsula between the Blue and White Niles is called the Gezira. It constitutes the great cotton-growing district of the Sudan, and possesses extensive irrigation works. Needless to say, rainfall is extremely vital to the Sudan. Its distribution varies and the vegetation belts of the country run accordingly; they run west-southwest and east-northeast.

According to Ruth McCreecy, the Sudan can be broken down into two zones: the Northern Sudan and the Southern Sudan. The northern area constitutes the Moslem section, mainly composed of Arabic tribes while the southern area is composed of Negroid peoples who are animistic in religion and speak various dialects. The geographical environment has molded the character traits of the Sudanese, said McCreecy. In her article on the Sudan, she pointed out:

All of the peoples of the Anglo-Egyptian Sudan have great physical endurance. This is

manifested not only in their fighting but also
in their hunting. They are 'absolutely fearless
in battle, placing little estimate on life, of
undaunted courage, and savage cruelty.'[7]

Moreover, McCreecy said that the Mohammedan or Arab is very stable emotionally. She
pointed to his lack of music as an indication of
his ability to achieve emotional satisfaction
without the accoutrements of the West. Yet, she
said:

> ...religious fervor as worked up by the dervish
> orders produces 'Holy Rollers' twice weekly
> in their groups. The chief agency seems to be
> self-hypnotism through rhythmic repetitions
> of the name, 'Allah.'[8]

The northern and southern zones of the Sudan
can be broken down along cultural, demographic,
and religious lines. Besides a Moslem north and
a Pagan south, there were great population
differences among the many tribes inhabiting the
Central Sudan.
       The population of the entire Sudan before
the advent of the Mahdia was estimated at
8,500,000.[9]   In 1905, due to the massacres,
diseases, and famines of the Khalifa's rule, it
fell to 1,853,000. Since then it has steadily
increased.[10]
       The tribes of the Sudan are divided into distinct
groups. At the time of the Mahdia, there were
four main tribal groups in the Central Sudan:
(1) the Kanuz; (2) the Fidaykiyya; (3) the Mahas,

and[4]   the Danaqla. According to Trimingham,
the Kanuz numbered 23,000 and occupied the
Egyptian territory between Aswan and Madig. The
Fidaykiyya, 30,000, occupied villages between
Korosko and Wadi Halfa. The Mahas lived in the
region Wadi Halfa—Dongola, and the Danaqla
people lived along the Nile from Dongola to Debba.
Of these four tribes, the Danaqla had the most
pronounced Hamitic features. Two other tribal
groups inhabited the central region beside these
four;[11]   these were the Shaiquiya and Ja'liya.
They, together with the Baggara of Kordofan,
provided the main host of the Mahdi's forces.

In the Red Sea Hills region dwelt the Beja
tribes, a truly Hamitic nomadic people. They
inhabited the eastern zone between the Nile, the
Atbara, and the Red Sea, to the eastern desert
and the hills north of Tokar. Trimingham said
that these tribes possessed a linguistic unity
peculiar to themselves. Further setting these
tribes off from the other tribes, Seligman said that
there were pronounced physical similarities between the Beja of the twentieth century with the
pre-dynastic Egyptian group.[12]

On the physical features of the Beja, Trimingham said:

> The physical features of the typical Beja are
> that they are moderately short, slightly-built
> men, with reddish-brown or brown skin...The
> face is usually long and oval...The nose is
> well-shaped and thoroughly Caucasian in type
> ...The hair is usually curly.[13]

The Beja are divided into four main tribal units; the *Bisharin*, *Ammar'ar*, *Hadendowa*, and *Beni-Amir*. The largest of the tribes, and the most virile, is the *Hadendowa*. This tribe's origins go back to 1600 A.D. when they conquered, intermarried with, or otherwise absorbed other similar tribes. The tribe became unified and consolidated under one Sheikh Musa ibn Ibrahim who was nazir during the Egyptian period. The *Hadendowa* live between Atbara and the Red Sea and their territory reaches as far south as the borders of Eritrea and Abyssinia.

The religion of the Beja, said Trimingham, "cannot be regarded as more than skin deep. None are particularly religious, though like most of the Sudanese they are extremely superstitious."[14]

When the Mahdi began his reign of conquest, the Beja tribes at first held themselves aloof. They ceased resistance to the Mahdi only when it became clear that the Mahdists were powerful enough to sweep all opposition before them. The Hadendowa then became the most feared and respected fighting men in the Mahdi's army.

The mass of the Mahdi's forces was comprised of *Baggara* tribesmen, fierce and loyal followers, and devout Moslems. It was these *Baggara* who captured the imagination of the English, and were dubbed "dervishes."

What was this force of Mahdism that brought these nomadic Sudanese tribes together under one banner? What were its origins? D.S. Margoliouth submitted an informative paper before the British Academy in 1915[15] in which he traced the

growth and development of Mahdism from its
earliest manifestations in the Moslem era beginning about 600 A.D. The main theme centers
around the idea of a Deliverer or Messianic
figure who would come to earth to lead his people
to new-found glory. It is not an altogether
exclusive notion, for the Hebrews and Christians
have also held these ideas of a resurrection and
a deliverance. Margoliouth said:

> The Christian, the Jewish, and the Islamic
> systems share the notion of an expected
> Deliverer who is to come and restore or
> adjust all things. They differ somewhat,
> however, in the formula employed. The
> Christian thinks of a Second Coming, the Jew
> of one who is to come, while the Islamic
> phrase is 'come forth' or 'rise up' suggestive
> of appearance after concealment or of rebellion
> against existing authority; for this latter notion
> is expressed in several Semitic languages by
> the word which signifies come out.[16]

In the Islamic order of things, the need for a
Mahdi was not apparent so long as the world was
in an orderly state. For about twenty-five years
after the death of the Prophet Mohammed, Islam
waged a successful "Holy War" against the
non-believers, but as soon as this hey-day of
victory was over, the force of Islam began levelling
off. After the death of the first Umayyad
sovereign, civil war broke out.[17]

The first Mahdi to appear in Arabian history,
according to the Arabic chronicler, Ibn Sa'd, was

Mohammed, son of Ali of the Alamid family.
Though Mohammed was not descended from the
Prophet, he was held in high esteem by the
Moslems.[18]   Margoliouth pointed out:

> The title, Mahdi, meaning 'guided', was not
> apparently taken by him, though, according to
> Ibn Sa'd, he had no objection to its being
> employed, whilst he preferred to be known by
> his name Mohammed or his patronymic Abu'l
> Kasim...[19]

There have been many predictions of the
coming of a Mahdi in Islamic writings. One
Islamic text reads:

> ...there appears to be another (etymology)
> which has not been without its influence on the
> history of Mahdism. One of Ibn Majul's
> traditions runs: 'The Prophet said certain
> persons shall come out from the East and
> prepare the way for the Mahdi.'[20]

Another text describes the coming of the
Mahdi.[21]   Margoliouth said:

> If the approach of the close of the first
> millenium was the signal for the appearance
> of a Mahdi, it would seem that the close of
> the first twelve hundred years led to similar
> expectations. (One of the prophecies of Abu
> Dawud said that: 'there shall come forth from
> Transoxania a man named al-Harith, whose
> vanguard shall be commanded by a man named

Mansur, who shall prepare the way for the
family of Mohammed, and it is incumbent on
all Moslems to obey and aid them.')[22]

In the case of all subsequent Mahdis, two
doctrines held true: (1) the self-professed Mahdi
was to claim membership in the Prophet's house
and (2) he was to emerge from obscurity. His
function was represented by the phrase: "he shall
fill the world with justice even as it is filled with
injustice..."[23]

As the years passed, Moslems grew dis-
satisfied with the secular lives of their rulers and
many returned to a life of denial, or asceticism.
Others prayed for a deliverer, or Mahdi who would
make the Islamic world pure once again. Sudanese
Mohammedanism bore a great deal of eschatological tradition.   It prophesied that in the last days
of the world there would appear a great redeemer,
one Mahdi, the "God-guided one."

The chiliastic kingdom of the Mahdi would then
be destroyed by the Dajjal (Anti-Christ) but the
Prophet Isa would return, kill the Dajjal,[24]
and fill the earth with justice by ruling according to the Law of Islam.[25]

The Mohammedan masses came to have a
passionate belief in the future deliverer, called
el-Mahdi.   Ibn Khaldun, the Arab historian,
explained this belief in his Muqaddama.

It is a universal belief amongst the Moslem
masses throughout the ages that at the End of

Time a man of the family of the Prophet must
manifest himself to confirm the faith and
proclaim justice. The Moslems will follow him
and he will establish his rule over the Islamic
Kingdoms. He will be called the Mahdi. The
appearance of the Dajjal after him and what
succeeds him are among the signs of the Hour
which are based on sound tradition. Isa will
either descend after the Mahdi and kill the
Dajjal, or He will descend with him and assist
at his killing. He will follow the Mahdi as
Imam in worship.[26]

There were presumed signs that would presage
the coming of the Mahdi. One was that he should
bear the same name as his ancestor, the Prophet,
Mohammed ibn 'Abd Allah, following the tradition,
"his name will be as my name and his father's
name as my father's name."[27]

The religion of the Mahdist state as set up by
Mohammed Ahmed had no basis for modern
church-state relationships. It was essentially a
primitive force, based on the notion of a spiritual
deliverer, and the destruction of the Anti-Christ
(Dajjal). As Trimingham said:

Since Islam does not distinguish between
church and state, the result has been that any
religious reformer must inevitably use political means, preach the jihad, not only against
polytheists but against other Moslems, and, if
successful, form a state...[28]

Mohammed Ahmed, the Mahdi, established the pattern for the Sudanese form of Mahdism. Trimingham described the Mahdi as a symbolic figure more than anything else:

> Mohammed Ahmed had been recreated through a profound spiritual crisis, and the Mahdia was the attempt to re-create in his own milieu the mutation which he had achieved in himself. [29]

The central and eastern Sudan rallied to the Mahdi because he symbolized deliverance to them. Through some miracle he, the supposed descendant of the Prophet Mohammed, would lead the Sudanese out of despair and want into a new era of glory. The unification of these tribes thus came about for religious reasons initially; political and economic conditions in the Sudan remained the deeper and long-range causes of the Mahdia.

It should be remembered that long years of corrupt Turko-Egyptian rule had not been able to unite the Sudanese against this form of political and economic oppression. As Trimingham so eloquently phrased it:

> It was religion which provided the stimulus though economic conditions determined the response. The result is that because Mohammed Ahmed has lived, because he stirred the Sudan to belief in a divine order, the Sudan can never be the same again. New factors have been brought into play in the psychology of the Sudanese which every administration must take

into account, and which have little to do with
the messianic expectations which were there
before and still color their lives.[30]

Who was this man, Mohammed Ahmed, who
succeeded in uniting the Sudanese tribes through
the force of Islam, and then, using their undaunted
warrior courage, carving a political state in the
Central Sudan?

Mohammed Ahmed was relatively young when
he assumed the Mahdiship of the Sudan. He was
under forty years of age. Born on August 12, 1849
in the province of Dongola, the son of a boat-
builder, he soon manifested a strong desire for
Islamic theological study. When his father,
Abdallah, died, three of his four sons followed his
trade. Mohammed, however, became the pupil of
Sheikh Mohammed al-Dikayr in the Gezira, and
later of Abdallah Khujih, near Berber. After his
religious training, Mohammed broke from the
usual path of advanced theological training, and
began a life of asceticism and mystical experiences. The followers of Sheikh al-Qurashi soon
recognized him as their new leader and made him
head of the Sammariya order. Still, it was not
until his announcement of the Mahdia that his power
reached its zenith. A Mahdi or "Guided One" was
expected to arise at the end of a century. At this
time, the thirteenth Moslem century was approaching its end.

Mohammed Ahmed assumed the Mahdiship
from strong personal conviction. Shouqair said
that:

A SLAVE CARAVAN IN THE SOUDAN.

Taken from: Gordon and the Mahdi: An Illustrated Narrative(1885)

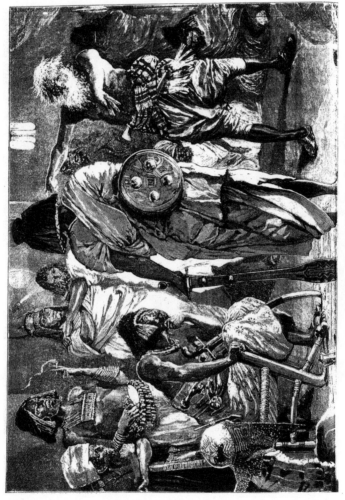

Dervish Preaching The Jihad, or Holy War, to Arab Chiefs

Beja tribesmen, of the Red Sea Hills. Men like these, the 'Fuzzy-Wuzzies' of Kipling's poem, were 'Uthman Diqna's warriors in the Mahdia.

ARRIVAL OF HICKS PASHA AND THE SOUDAN FIELD FORCE AT SUAKIM.

HIS HIGHNESS ISMAIL PASHA (From a Photograph taken in 1867).

Arabi Pasha

Chaillé-Long Bey

GENERAL GORDON.

...on his return from al-Masallamiya to Abba,
Mohammed Ahmed began to study the tra-
ditional prophecies of the Mahdi and to apply
them to himself.   The conviction of the
Mahdiship took the form of a vision or series
of visions and Mohammed Ahmed communi-
cated the secret of his divine election first to
Abdullahi and then to his other disciples and
adherents in Rabi II 1298 (March, 1881).[31]

The great manifestation of Mohammed as the
Mahdi was made on the island of Abba.   This
occurred on I Shu'ban 1298 (June 29, 1881) when
Mohammed Ahmed dispatched communiqués to
various notables, assuming the title of Mohammed
el-Mahdi.   The most important aspects of the
Mahdi's communiqués were the call to a jihad and
hijra. Holt said:

The duty he urges upon his followers is the
hijra, the flight for the Faith from among the
infidels to the Mahdi. The call to the hijra is
the earliest example of a conscious parallel
between the career of the Prophet and that of
the Mahdi, of which we shall find other
examples during his mission. But the Mahdi's
use of prophetic parallels was not a blind
antiquarianism.   He and his followers were
deliberately reenacting in their own persons
the sufferings and the triumphs of the early
days of Islam and their consciousness of
playing a part in this great drama was an
inspiration to them.[32]

Perhaps the most authoritative description of Mohammed Ahmed was that of Father Joseph Ohrwalder, the clergyman who was imprisoned by the Mahdi for ten years (1882-1892) and who wrote an illuminating commentary on the various aspects of the Mahdi's reign.

Of his physical appearance and personal character, Ohrwalder said:

> His outward appearance was strongly fascinating; he was a man of strong constitution, very dark complexion, and his face always wore a pleasant smile, to which he had by long practice accustomed himself. Under this smile gleamed a set of singularly white teeth, and between the two upper middle ones was a v-shaped space, which in the Sudan is considered a sign that the owner will be lucky. His mode of conversation too had by training become exceptionally pleasant and sweet. As a messenger of God, he pretended to be in direct communication with the Deity. All orders which he gave were supposed to have come to him by inspiration, and it became therefore a sin to refuse to obey them; disobedience to the Mahdi's orders was tantamount to resistance to the will of God, and was therefore punishable by death.[33]

Mohammed Ahmed's greatest power lay in his unyielding belief that he was the expected Mahdi of Allah. His personality was strong, his voice was well trained, by years of practice, to delivering religious orations. Mohammed's simple

asceticism was not unlike the type that many
other holy men engaged in, except for one basic
difference. He absolutely believed himself to be
the Mahdi and acted accordingly, proclaiming
the millenium to the masses, and receiving their
obedient response to his divine call. Margoliouth
said that Mohammed was the most recent in a long
line of self-styled Mahdis. His prominence in
history lies in the fact that he was among the most
successful of them:

> The Mahdi who has acquired the greatest fame
> is that Mohammed Ahmed who, between the
> years 1881 and 1885, troubled the Sudan, and
> left his successor, a mighty empire...This
> personage claimed to be the twelfth Imam, the
> Mohammed born Hasan al-Askari, who for
> more than ten centuries had been in hiding,
> though at times, as we have seen, changing his
> refuge. A peculiarity about the line which he
> adopted was that he endeavored to reproduce
> the career of the Prophet Mohammed by having
> a hijra (hegira) or migration, and four lieu-
> tenants, which indicate a curious conception of
> the meaning of the word, Khalifa; one of these
> became famous as his successor... [34]

Professor Holt considers the Mahdist movement of 1881 to have had its roots in political,
social, and economic ferment as well as religious
fervor. What the Mahdi accomplished, claims
Holt, was a political revolution. It amounted,
essentially, to the overthrow of Egyptian rule and
the establishment of an indigenous Islamic state.

What Holt means is that, although the Mahdist
state's immediate manifestation was a religious
unit, its ultimate goal was that of a sovereign
political state.   Hence, from a messianic com-
munity, the Mahdia grew into a political and
military autocracy.   The Mahdia went through two
main phases: (1) the era of Mohammed Ahmed,
the Mahdi, and (2) the empire period of Abdullahi
who succeeded the Mahdi with the title of Khalifat
al-Mahdi ("Successor of the Mahdi") in 1885.[35]

The Mahdi continued propagating his ideas
throughout the year, 1881. He appealed, particularly, to the superstitious nature of the Sudanese
tribes, manifesting openly before all, such signs
of "prophecy" as a mole on his right cheek, and
doctoring up such holy sites as Jabal Massa. He
performed a hijra to Jabal Qadir in the Nuba
Mountains which he renamed Jabal Massa in line
with the idea that the Mahdi would arise from that
hill where the people would swear everlasting
faith in him.[36]   When he felt ready, he stepped
into the midst of the masses and announced his
claim to Mahdiship.   In his manifesto to the
people of Khartoum he wrote:

> All that I have told you of my succession to the
> Mahdia was told to me by the Lord of Being
> (the Prophet) when I was awake and in good
> health, free from all transgressions of the
> Law...enjoying a sound mind, keeping to the
> sunnar of the Prophet, adhering to what he
> ordered and avoiding what he forbade. [37]

In another religious decree, Mohammed described the meaning of his coming to the Sudan as

a combination of pious ascetic and dynamic
avenger.

> As God had preordained to confer upon His
> humble slave the highest succession (Khalifa)
> from God and His Prophet, the Prophet told me
> that I am the awaited Mahdi and appointed me
> to succeed him by repeatedly making me sit in
> his chair in the presence of the four khalifas,
> the Quths and al-Khidir. God helped me with
> His favorite angels, with the saints both living
> and dead from Adam to this day and likewise
> with the believing jinn. In time of war the
> Prophet appears in person with them before
> my army; likewise, the Khalifa, the Quths and
> al-Khidir. He gave me the Sword of Victory,
> and I was told that no one, not even the
> Thaqalan (mankind and jinnkind), can defeat
> me when it is with me. The Prophet said to
> me: 'God has made for you a Sign of Mahdi-
> ship', and it is the mole on my right cheek.
> He made for me another sign as well—a banner
> of light will appear and will be with me in time
> of war and Azra'il will carry it. God will
> strengthen my friends with it and fear will
> descend into the hearts of my enemies.[38]

Mohammed issued a further decree that the
name, darawish[39] (anglicized—dervish) should
be changed to ansar. The name ansar was
supposed to represent a more pious and ascetic
people. Darawish, translated from the Arabic,
means "poor man." The Mahdi wanted his
followers to represent not merely pious and

simple people, but intelligent and far-seeing
individuals, and defenders of Allah's cause. The
decree read:

> All the faithful have already been cautioned not
> to call themselves *darawish* but *ansar,* that is
> to say, those whose hearts are entirely
> consecrated to God and whose souls have
> become enlightened by a desire to possess the
> joys of this world to come, quitting the
> pleasures of this life and having full faith in
> the power of the Almighty who has created
> Paradise for those who are truly faithful to
> Him. [40]

In the first two years of the Mahdi's rise to
power, his real political and military potential was
evaluated by Consul Zaghrab who relayed his
observations to Earl Granville. In essence, what
Zaghrab said was that the Mahdi represented a
real and imminent danger not only to England's
interests in Egypt and the Sudan, but to European
interests throughout the Middle East. The force
of Islam coupled with the growing unrest en-
gendered by Egyptian and Turkish misrule, provided the political and religious fuel for a great
jihad.   Consul Zaghrab, in his communiqué to
Granville dated, St. Thomas, December 22, 1883,
wrote:

> The man Mohammed Ahmed, who has assumed
> the title of the 'Mahdi' has come forward just
> at the time it was foretold he should appear,
> and his acts have been so strictly in accordance

with what was prophesied about him that they cannot fail to impress at least the lower class of Moslems, and lead them to believe that he is the true Mahdi...

The advent of the Mahdi, whose mission is to purify and restore Islam, has come at a time when the Moslem mind is strongly alarmed and agitated, and he will, if he is not speedily put down, become the center or focus of the hopes and aspirations of the Mohammedan world and, though a mere imposter, he will nevertheless become formidable, for enthusiasts from all parts will come to his standard.[41]

According to Winston Churchill, the Arabs of the Sudan who fought under the banner of the Mahdi and later, under that of his disciple, the Khalifa Abdullahi, did so for different reasons during the course of the Mahdist state.

...the Arabs who destroyed Yusef, who assaulted El Obeid, who annihilated Hicks, fought in the glory of religious zeal; that the Arabs who opposed Graham, Earle, and Stewart fought in defense of the soil; and that the Arabs who were conquered by Kitchener fought in the pride of an army. Fanatics charged at Shaykan; patriots at Abu Klea; warriors at Omdurman.[42]

The Mahdi, further, attempted to turn the clock back to the era of the Prophet Mohammed. His proclamations revealed an overwhelming asceticism coupled with a fanatical spirit of self-

sacrifice. It was just this type of emotional
message that appealed to the Sudanese Moslems:

> In the name of God the Compassionate and
> Merciful, praise be to God our gracious Lord,
> and prayer and peace upon our Prince Mo-
> hammed and his followers!
> From the zealous servant of his Lord, Mo-
> hammed the Mahdi, son of Abdullah, to his
> friends in God, to the faithful who believe in
> God and in His Book...God hath said, 'Family
> and children will not profit you in the day of
> resurrection...'
> The Government now is just as it was in the
> days of the Prophet, and our times are as those
> of the Prophet, etcetera. [43]

Mohammed Ahmed had a particular grievance
against the Turks whom he considered as trans-
gressors of God's apostles and prophets. His
proclamation on this matter exhibits the hatred
he felt for the Turks and their treatment of the
Sudanese people:

> Verily these Turks thought that theirs was the
> kingdom and the command of (God's) apostles
> and of His prophets and of him who commanded
> them to imitate them. They judged by other
> than God's revelation (the Koran) and altered
> the Shari'a of Our Lord Mohammed, the
> Apostle of God, and insulted the Faith of God
> and place poll-taxes (al-jizza) on your necks
> together with the rest of the Moslems...
> Verily the Turks used to drag away your men

and imprison them in fetters and take captive
your women and your children and slay
unrighteously the soul under God's protection.
In all this they had no mercy upon the small
among you nor respect for the great among
you.[44]

The Mahdi went on to win victories for his
ansar. As he did so, the Egyptian soldiers began
fighting with an uneasy conscience.   Perhaps it
seemed to them that Mohammed Ahmed was,
indeed, the awaited Mahdi and that they were
blaspheming against Allah by fighting the descendant of the Prophet.[45]

The *Baggara* tribes of the south of Darfur were
the first to rally behind the banner of the Mahdi.
They were destined to become the vanguard of his
army of redemption. Like the other tribes of the
Sudan, the *Baggara* faced the exorbitant taxation
of the Egyptian administration and grew rebellious
against the corrupt regime of the Egyptians and
Turks.   From 1881 to 1883 the Mahdi rallied his
great host: the *Baggara* of Kordofan, the *kababish*
and other camel-owning tribes of the north, and
the *Hadendowa* and other Beja groups of the Red
Sea Hills.

The seeds of revolt had been sown by Egyptian
misgovernment and Turkish corruption in the
Sudan tax agencies. The rebellion burst forth in
1881 in a fanatical Islamic movement. Though its
deep-rooted causes were political and economic,
its immediate manifestation and popular appeal
was religious. For the next five years, the Mahdi

was to gain such power and prestige in the Sudan as to threaten British overland lines of communication to her East Asian possessions, and the British occupation government in Lower Egypt.

CHAPTER

4

Political and Military Synthesis: The Sword of Islam

L'insurrection du Mahdi, la prise d'Obeid, le désastre de Hicks, la révolte d'Arabi, l'occupation anglaise de l'Égypte, le retour dramatique de Gordon au Soudan, la prise de Khartoum, le protectorat de Zanzibar et cette burlesque expédition pour secourir un pacha égyptien ne sont aussi que des incidents de ces faiblesses inconscientes, plus terribles qu'un drame, qu' éclaire de ses lueurs lugubres l'incendie d' Alexandrie.

— Colonel Chaillé-Long in L'Égypte et ses provinces perdues

We took our chanst among the Kyber 'ills,
The Boers knocked us silly at a mile,
The Burman gave us Iriwaddy chills,
An' a Zulu impi dished us up in style:
But all we ever got from such as they
Was pop to what the Fuzzy made us swaller;
We 'eld our bloomin' own, the papers say,
But man for man, the Fuzzy knocked us'oller.
...So 'ere's to you, Fuzzy-Wuzzy, at your 'ome in the Soudan;
You're a poor benighted 'eathen but a first-class fightin' man —

—from Rudyard Kipling's "Fuzzy-Wuzzy"

CHAPTER

4

Political and Military Synthesis: The Sword of Islam

Harold Temperley, the famed British historian,[1] says that Gladstone's actions in Egypt and the Sudan were definitely not part of long-range policy but came about because of circumstances. Gladstone, he contends, sought to follow a foreign policy of restriction and consolidation rather than one of expansion and added responsibilities.

He wished to restrict rather than to increase, responsibilities and territorial obligations; he was anxious not to come into conflict with foreign Powers; he desired to encourage and not to repress national movements wherever they manifested themselves. The Egyptian adventure, therefore, violated the fundamental principles of his policy.[2]

What prompted England to finally occupy Egypt and subsequently to move into the Sudan

was a young revolutionary movement led by
Colonel Arabi of the Egyptian Army. Disguised
under the color of a military revolt, it was in
reality a full-scale Egyptian national movement
which proved an imminent danger to the Khedive.
Even more realistically, the English soon saw the
real financial instability of Egypt. Gladstone had
always maintained that the obligations of governments to their debtors was a sacred trust. Hence,
when the Egyptians repudiated their debts in 1875,
he described it as "the greatest of political
crimes."[3]

While England could coerce Turkey, she could
not use the same measures with Egypt. Earlier,
Lord Canning had established it as a principle
which Palmerston later adhered to, that, "the
contraction of a loan by a British Government
with an undeveloped Power was undesirable
because it ultimately involved interference with
internal affairs."[4]

Gladstone was forced to adopt unorthodox
political moves in Egypt to consolidate orthodox
financial interests. Military intervention in 1882
was one of the methods employed. Before this,
however, there had been growing signs of a move
toward internal interference by England. In one
sense, both France and England were responsible
for the crisis that led to an Arab uprising in
Egypt, and an Islamic revival in the Sudan. When
the Gambetta administration (November, 1881 to
January, 1882) fell, Bismarck interposed to break
up any further Anglo-French cooperation. The
Khedive was given a brief reprieve. Meanwhile,
Arabi Pasha's national movement grew in in-

tensity. Both Britain and France sent squadrons to Alexandria to meet the threat of internal anarchy and strife. The European situation was, in turn, altered by this turn of events.

Lord Salisbury, in 1887, said in plain words: "I heartily wish we had never gone into Egypt. Had we not done so, we could snap our fingers at all the world." [5]

This was a frank evaluation of the European situation. So long as Anglo-French rivalries continued in Egypt, just so long could the other European Powers apply pressure on England. Among the scheming European leaders was the redoubtable Bismarck who sought to keep France and England apart as well as Russia and thus to secure France's diplomatic isolation in a European world of alliances and alignments.

In 1883 the financial situation in Egypt grew critical with the added expense of the Sudanese campaign against the Mahdi. This added economic burden on England's resources raised a storm of protest at Westminster where the "Consolidationists" fought with the forward wing of the British "Expansionist" school. In the meantime, several thousand miles to the east, British-trained forces were meeting bitter defeats at the hands of the rising military power of Mohammed el-Mahdi. Beginning in Central Kordofan, the Guided One led his Ansar east, west, and north to conquer the territories of Darfur, Dongola, the Red Sea Hills, and the populated fringes of the great Bayuda Desert.

One of the prime causes of corruption and misrule in this dry land was the institution of slavery. It provided the corrupt slavers and ivory traders with a new source of wealth. These entrepreneurs in human misery made their own laws; and most of them were applied by force. General Gordon had seen the direct encouragement of the slave trade in the Sudan; slavers worked hand in hand with high government officials. The slave trade flourished in the provinces of Bahr el-Ghazal, Darfur, and Kordofan. According to Moorehead, at least 5,000 traders were operating in these areas at the time of Khedive Ismail's rule.[6]   Romolo Gessi had estimated that "since 1860, when the traffic began, more than 400,000 women and children had been taken from the area to be sold in Egypt and Turkey, and that many thousands more had died."[7]

Dr. Schweinfurth, the Baltic explorer and naturalist, described conditions in the provinces as appalling. He felt that unless something drastic were done, the African tribes would be entirely wiped out. Wrote Schweinfurth, "The kindest thing that the enlightened ruler of Egypt can do for these lands is to leave them alone."[8]

Gordon established a new staff for these provinces which included some extraordinary personalities. Among them were Romolo Gessi, appointed governor of Bahr el-Ghazal with the rank of Pasha, Rudolf Carl von Slatin, a young Viennese officer appointed to Darfur, Frank Lupton, a young Englishman who was being trained for special duties at Khartoum, and Edward Schnitzer, a Prussian who was appointed governor

of the Equatorial Province in 1879 by Gordon,
taking on the name of Emin Pasha. In 1884, after
being cut off from Khartoum for more than a year,
Emin Pasha held out stubbornly against the
dervish forces. By 1886, he received a letter
from Nubar Pasha urging him to withdraw his
garrison, in view of the fall of Khartoum, and
"sauve qui peut." [9]

The political-military considerations in the
Sudan depended in very large part on one Evelyn
Baring, a powerful British figure in the fields of
high finance and politics. Gordon considered
Baring a patrician thorn in his side. The debates
that raged in 1884-1885 on the subject of a relief
column to break the Mahdi's siege of Khartoum
must have seen Gordon sitting pensively in the
palace at Khartoum contemplating Baring's "practical position" of the financial soundness of such
an expedition. Even his less inhibited colleagues
wrote of Baring:

> The virtues of Patience are known,
> But I think that, when put to the touch,
> The people of Egypt will own with a groan,
> There's an Evil in Baring too much. [10]

However, Khartoum was yet the last phase in
the initial expansion of Sudanese Islam under the
Mahdi. Three years earlier, in 1882, British
intervention forces first met and clashed with the
vanguard of the Mahdi's army. Before this clash,
the British had scored a resounding victory over
the Egyptian Army on September 13, 1882 at
Tel-el-Kebir, about sixty-five miles from Cairo.

General Wolseley with a force of 20,000 men brought the action to a close in several hours and entered Cairo in triumph. The British occupation of Egypt was secured.

After Tel-el-Kebir, the English, flushed with recent victory, prepared to move rapidly against what seemed, on the surface, a minor revolt in the Sudan led by a religious zealot. They greatly underestimated his power and prestige. As Moorehead eloquently says:

> Like a sandstorm in the desert he appears, suddenly and inexplicably out of nowhere, and by some strange process of attraction generates an ever-increasing force as he goes along. [11]

The Mahdi phrased his goal simply to his followers: "Kill the Turks and cease to pay taxes." To the nomadic tribes of the desert, rule by any settled government was hateful. Especially despised was the corrupt Egyptian administration. Tribal uprisings began early in 1882 and spread rapidly throughout the Central Sudan. At first, these local risings were dealt with effectively by the Egyptians, but soon they became difficult to contain. To make matters more difficult, the great distances between some of these tribal risings made the movement of government troops a logistical hardship. According to Holt, this constituted the first phase of the Mahdi's movements. The second phase, he says, opened with the arrival of a Mahdist army in the province (Kordofan). This, combined with more general tribal risings, tried the Turko-Egyptian forces to the utmost. In pitched battles they were still usually victorious, but they were unable to consolidate their successes and had to withdraw to their fortified bases, which, in the third phase, were gradually reduced by the Ansar. In Kordofan, by the autumn of 1882, only two garrisons still held out, at Bara and El Obeid.[12]

At the end of August, 1882, the Mahdi moved against the two towns. On the road to El Obeid, he detached a small force to capture some Austrian missionaries at Dilling. Among them was one Father Joseph Ohrwalder who was an eye-witness to the siege of El Obeid and who remained a prisoner of the Mahdi for ten years. After his escape, Ohrwalder wrote one of the best contemporary accounts of the early years of the Mahdist movement, Ten Years' Captivity in the Mahdi's Camp. It was translated by F. R. Wingate.[13] As he marched, the Mahdi's forces grew until in September, he camped just outside of El Obeid with perhaps 30,000 warriors.

El Obeid was the second largest city in the Sudan after Khartoum. It was the center of a prospering trade in gum, ostrich feathers, cattle, skins, and senna. In the city, even the wealthiest of the traders were secretly sympathetic with the cause of the Mahdi. His capture of the town was in no small measure due to the cooperation of these sympathizers. Mohammed Sa'id Pasha, the

governor residing in El Obeid, reinforced the inner
and outer walls of the town and garrisoned them
with his small force. The governor tried to inspire
confidence in the townspeople of his ability
successfully to defend the city, but the wiser of
them saw the writing on the wall and deserted to
the Mahdi.

On the 8th of September, the Mahdi launched a
full-scale frontal assault on the garrison. His
Ansar succeeded in capturing the outer wall but
were met with a withering barrage of fire when
they tried to storm the inner citadel. At length
the Mahdi was forced to withdraw his remaining
forces. The battle of El Obeid taught the Mahdi a
valuable lesson. Theobald said:

> This reverse undoubtedly made a deep im-
> pression on the Mahdi. It was the first time
> he had forsaken his previous tactics of
> surprise and ambush; the first time he had
> experienced the devastating power of firearms
> in the hands of determined defenders...He
> drew off his forces and did not renew the
> attack. He ordered that never again should a
> direct assault be made on a fortified city,
> defended by a fresh and well-armed garrison.
> He prepared to reduce the town by siege and
> starvation.[14]

El Obeid fell soon after, and Mohammed Ahmed
was venerated as the greatest of the prophets by
his followers. Father Ohrwalder, in his manuscript,[15]   wrote that the Mahdi was held in as
high esteem as the Prophet himself. The water

which he used to wash himself was distributed among his <u>Ansar</u> who hoped to find in it potent cures for their ills. The Mahdi, flushed by this first great victory, announced that,

> when all the Sudan had fallen, he would take Egypt and proceed to the bloodiest of all battles outside Mecca. Next, he would advance on Jerusalem where Christ would descend from heaven to meet him, and Islam thereafter would conquer the whole world. [16]

When the Mahdi spoke of the whole world, it was the world of the Sudanese, Egyptian, and Arabian deserts that he meant. The desert was, indeed, the only world that these people knew. As Moorehead says:

> The Mahdi smiled and a sublime confidence radiated from him. He was not at all dismayed when he heard, in the summer months of 1883, that an Egyptian army commanded by a British general was advancing upon him from the Nile. [17]

Before launching into the Hicks' expedition it is well to consider the effect that the fall of El Obeid had on the other tribes of the Sudan, notably the <u>Beja</u> tribes of the Red Sea Hills. When the revolt first began, the <u>Beja</u> tribes were little affected. Their language and way of life were different from the Arab Sudanese, and they remained isolated politically and culturally from the tribes of the Central Sudan. In the summer of 1883, the Mahdi sent an emissary to the Bejas, summoning them to the Holy War. His messenger was Uthman Diqna. (Anglicized as Osman Digna.) Digna was a citizen of Suakin, an important port city in the eastern Sudan, and was himself partially of Beja descent. Among the Beja, the tribe which provided the vanguard of Osman Digna's forces was the *Hadendowa*. Holt says that the decisive factor in bringing the *Hadendowa* over to the ranks of the Mahdi was not the personality of Digna, but an alliance that was consummated between Osman and Sheikh al-Tahir al-Tayyib al-Majdhub, the local chief of the Sufi order which had its head-quarters[18]   at El Damer.[19]

Thus, by swearing allegiance to the Mahdi and recognizing Osman Digna as his delegate to the Beja, Sheikh al-Tahir brought to the Mahdist ranks a fanatical fighting force. Within several months, communication lines between Berber and Suakin were cut, Egyptian forces were met and defeated at Tokar on the Red Sea coast, and the Bejas prepared to meet further Egyptian rein-forcements moving up the Nile to Suakin.

At this time, the Mahdi, realizing that the ensuing battles would be long and arduous, instructed his Emirs as well as the loyal Ansar to don the sacred *jibba*. The *jibba* was a rough cotton shirt that stretched to the knees; under it the Mahdist trooper wore long drawers reaching to the ankles; on his feet he wore either sandals, or nothing at all; on his head he wore a skull-cap, with a turban wound around it. As this uniform felt the wear and tear of long marches and combat, it had to be patched; this patched outfit

soon became the official standard uniform of the
Mahdist army. Why did the Mahdi insist on such
a puritanical outfit for the glorious army of the
Prophet?   Theobald has offered a clear answer:

> In all this there was nothing remarkable. The
> Mahdi was merely expressing in terms ap-
> propriate to his environment a Puritan attitude
> to life whose essential features do not vary
> greatly from age to age, or country to country.
> He was speaking a language that Cromwell's
> Ironsides in seventeenth century England and
> Ibn Sa'ud's Wahhabis in present-day Arabia
> would equally understand and approve. Simi-
> larly, although the penalties for infringements
> of his rules may sound mercilessly harsh to
> those accustomed to the careful gradations of
> fines and imprisonments imposed by modern
> law courts, they were understood and accepted
> as the correct application of Sar'ia law by
> his own people. [20]

Perhaps Theobald's analogy with Cromwell
was a bit extreme, but it is quite evident that
asceticism and the idea of renunciation of the
material world were the key personal principles
of the Mahdi, and he applied them as well to his
military forces.

In 1883, although he had gained several
impressive victories, the Mahdi had not yet
developed a well-structured administration in the
areas he had overrun. This was probably due to
the rapidity of his advance and the lack of time to
organize the provinces. Besides, several stra-

tegic British bases still operated in the Sudan:
Khartoum, Suakin, Berber, Trinkitat, and Korosko.
So long as these bases existed the Mahdi could not
wait to consolidate his gains.   It was left to the
administration of his disciple, Khalifa Abdullahi,
to reconstitute the boundaries, and government
of a Mahdist state.

The Mahdi's army was constituted on the
basis of his four Khalifas, who were appointed
by him and who were to correspond to the four
Companions and successors of the Prophet.   The
Khalifas were Abd Allahi, Ali wad Hilu, and
Mohammed al-Shauf.   The last position was
offered to the leader of the Sanusi sect of Algeria
but was refused.   For the remainder of the
Mahdiship, the position remained vacant.   Each
Khalifa was the nominal leader of a section of the
army with his own emblem. [21]

While the Khalifas headed the army sections,
the strategy and tactics, and logistical planning
was left to the veteran Emirs. [22]

By 1883, the British government was informed
of the growing strength of the Mahdi and the
imminent need for a show of force.   The official
communiqué from Consul Moncrieff to Earl
Granville read as follows:

I Have the honor to forward for your Lordship's information a copy of a dispatch which
I have addressed to Sir E. Malet on the subject
of a movement in the East Sudan in favor of
the so called Mahdi...It is probable...that
while two leaders of the insurrection called
Mohammed Tahir and Osman Digna remain at

large, the roads will be insecure, and it would,
I think, become the Egyptian Government to
send at least such portion as can be spared of
the reinforcements requested by Tewfik Bey. . .
In Suakin there are 100 infantry, partly made
up of convicts, and there are 6 Krupp guns
without special artillerymen. In Tokar there
are 150 such as in Suakin, and a mountain-gun.
The above force is insufficient to impress the
natives with an idea that they cannot overcome
the Government.

I have, & c.
(Signed) Lyneloch N. Moncrieff [23]

One of the most bitter battles was fought in the
Eastern Sudan against the *Hadendowa* at a place
called Tamaii. It was this place that Rudyard
Kipling made famous in his poem on the so-called
"Fuzzy-Wuzzies." John Gordon, one of the
participants in this struggle, described the battle
in his memoirs, My Six Years With the Black
Watch. [24] He began with a logistical survey of
the military movements, and then went into the
fighting itself. At Suakin, Gordon said, his unit
spent two days unloading provisions and ammunition in preparation for an advance upon the
Bejas' position at Tamaii. His unit, the Black
Watch, was ordered to march ahead of the rest
of the army to guard these supplies. [25] According to Gordon, the infantry were formed into two
squares. The first square was comprised of the
Second Brigade together with the Black Watch;
seven-hundred yards behind the first square
stood the second square, composed of the First

Brigade. Gordon's description of the action was
fast and furious. He gave the psychological as
well as the military view of close combat:

> We had marched over the plain not far when
> we received the command, 'Fix bayonets',
> then 'charge'. Forward we dashed there being
> nothing to check us except a few stunted
> shrubs; the enemy's outposts had been driven
> in by our mounted infantry and some Abyssinian
> scouts that accompanied us. A, B, and C
> companies were in line, D company halted at
> the edge of the ravine. D company wheeled to
> the left, thereby forming the left front angle
> of the first square, just in time to meet the
> first mad rush of the Sudanese from their
> concealment in the ravine where they had been
> waiting like ravenous beasts of prey. Our
> front rank kneeling and rear rank standing, we
> poured the volleys into the hordes as they
> continued to rise out of the ravine. From the
> other side, across the wide stretch of stony
> river-bed, they constantly advanced; pictur-
> esquely formidable they were, led by their
> sheikhs on horseback. We soon discovered
> that if we killed or wounded a sheikh, eight men
> would leave the fighting line to carry him off
> the field. We took advantage of this, picking
> off every sheikh we could and firing volleys at
> his attendants, thus making a new set of eight
> attendants leave the line to carry him off. [26]

As the fighting continued, these Beja tribesmen
relentlessly pushed forward, engaging the British

troops in hand-to-hand combat. The smoke and din grew in intensity. Gordon described the scene dramatically:

> The struggle developed into a wild hand-to-hand contest between swords, spears, crooked knives, and boomerangs on the one side and bayonets on the other, a veritable hell. The smoke from our Martinis hung over us, a dense cloud, not a breath of air stirring to carry it away.
>
> Just how long this mad contest had raged I do not know, —time was of no consequence—when suddenly our officers and non-commissioned officers forming the supernumerary rank, were attacked from the rear. Great God, the center of our square was filled with the fiends. Clean them out, that was the only thing to do and with bayonet; to fire would be to shoot our own men. Foes in front, foes in rear! Our move was to fall back with the rear rank and officers fighting those in the center of the square while the front rank engaged those still pressing hard on us, sticking to us like burs. We kept trimming their ranks... [27]

The battle was more or less evenly matched until the British committed the First Brigade in support of the Black Watch. Then, the picture changed and victory became assured. As John Gordon pointed out:

> ...we again advanced to retake lost ground; but we were an entirely different regiment; the

strain, the tenseness of close action, had used
up all reserve power. I remember feeling
utterly weak from incessant use of the bayonet.
We had been at it two hours; from nine to
eleven the struggle of the broken square lasted.
The First Brigade,[28] without much resistance,
captured the camp of the leader, Osman Digna.
Thus ended the battle of Tamaii.[29]

THE CORNER OF A BRITISH SQUARE IN THE SOUDAN.

CAPTURING THE ENEMY'S SUPPLIES IN THE DESERT.

The turning point in the Mahdi's rise to political and military power was the battle of
Shaykan. It was in this engagement that a large
ill-equipped native force defeated a compact
modern army under British officers. How this
was done has been ably described by A. B.
Theobald in his book, The Mahdiya . There
weren't many living eye-witnesses to the engagement after the Mahdi's victory, and so Theobald's
thesis is based largely on official communiqués

and military directives up to the collapse of
Colonel Hicks' Army of the Sudan.

In January, 1883, Colonel Hicks, a British
officer, was appointed Chief of Staff of the Army
of the Sudan. Hicks' background was impressive.
He had been a career officer in the Indian Army
where he had seen action during the Sepoy Mutiny;
he had been with the British expedition to Abyssinia. Yet, despite these military experiences,
Hicks had little personal experience at command-
ing troops in the field. Suddenly, he found himself
facing the new responsibilities of desert warfare.

In September, 1883, the army under Hicks
marched out from El Dueim in square formation
with the baggage and stores in the center of the
square. Such a huge, cumbersome body traveling across the Sudan could not help but offer a
tempting target to the enemy. As the army
entered Shat, great disorder developed. Unit
commanders could not locate their respective
units, and orders were misinterpreted. It is no
wonder that Colonel Hicks started his campaign
on the wrong pathway. At a special meeting held
by the principal officers, Alu al-Din Pasha asked
for a basic change of plan. He advocated that,
instead of establishing supply posts [30]   along
the army's route of advance, it should carry
fifty-days supply of food with it and sever communications with its base. In such a way, the
Egyptian officer argued, the army would not be
hampered by a long supply line which would be
inefficient in convoying supplies to the advance
elements, and would create unnecessary deploy-
ment of army detachments to guard these supply

posts. Instead, the army, cut loose from its base of operations, could fight as a self-sustaining unit, concentrating on offensive operations without worry as to its material support. Alu al-Din Pasha's plan was foolhardy. It involved unnecessary risks such as cutting an entire army off from its base of supplies, advancing into unfamiliar terrain without adequate reconnaissance, and incorporating a dual command between Hicks Pasha and the senior Egyptian officer, Husain Pasha. As Theobald stated:

> The historian cannot but marvel again at the lack of foresight, of knowledge, of preparation, revealed by this hasty council. [31]

Meanwhile, the Mahdi had not been idle. Spies brought him daily reports of the movements of Hicks' army. After Hicks had left El Dueim, the Mahdi sent 3,000 men under the Emirs Abd al-Halim and Abu Qarja to move to within one day's march from Hicks and destroy all the wells along his route of advance. In this way, the Mahdi hoped to weaken and demoralize the Egyptian force before meeting it in full-scale battle. Holt says that the expedition was doomed from the start. The disagreements between Hicks and his Egyptian colleagues, the lack of water for the army, and the holy proclamations of the Mahdi which were scattered along the route of march all succeeded in demoralizing and so, weakening, the force. [32]

No reliable account is available of the last days of Hicks' army, except for the stories told by a few survivors, including Hicks Pasha's

cook. According to these accounts, on the 3rd of
November, the army moved towards Kashgil.
After marching for ten miles, they camped behind
a zareba.[33]   According to Theobald:

> The next morning—it was a Sunday—the march
> was resumed; and before an hour had passed,
> the Mahdists suddenly attacked the rear of
> the square. A few penetrated, but the front
> face, wheeling round the flanks, came to the
> support of the rear and the attack was driven
> off. Unfortunately, many of those carrying
> water fell outside the square, and it was
> impossible to recover the water-skins in the
> face of the heavy fire.[34]

On November 5th, 1883, the army assumed
a different formation, one lead square and two
flanking squares with transport and stores in
their respective centers. The squares were
separated by some 300 yards forming a huge
triangle as they advanced. They had been
marching about an hour when, according to the
survivors of the engagement,

> ...a whirlwind attack was launched on the
> first square. The others opened fire in-
> discriminately on friend and foe alike. In
> a few minutes the first square was swept
> away; and the second and the third in turn.
> Thirsty, sleepless, weary, demoralized, they
> could make little resistance.[35]

Except for one or two-hundred who lived to be the Mahdi's prisoners, Hicks' army was decimated.   The first great defeat had been dealt the Anglo-Egyptian forces in the Sudan at the battle of Shaykan.

Back in Cairo, Sir Evelyn Baring sent an urgent message regarding the serious Sudan situation to Earl Granville.   In it he discussed the imminent dangers awaiting British interests in Egypt if the Mahdi insurrection were to reach Khartoum and then veer northward in its revolutionary course.   The significant section of this message read:

> If General Hicks' army is destroyed, it is nearly certain that the Egyptian Government will lose the whole of the Sudan, unless some assistance from outside is given to them; and once they begin to withdraw, it is hard to say at what point along the valley of the Nile they could stem the rebel movement. [36]

The British realized that if Hicks were to fall, nothing would stop the Mahdi from advancing on Khartoum.   If he could take this city, all the wavering tribes in the surrounding region would unequivocally flock to his standard.   When news was received of the Hicks disaster at Shaykan, the British government rested its last hopes for the retention of the Sudan on General Charles Gordon.   Gordon was a man of rare talents.   He possessed great physical courage coupled with a talent for military command and administration. Like other English "greats", he belonged to that

school of military leaders and statesmen which
included Winston Churchill and T. E. Lawrence.

Gordon was at Khartoum in 1884, having
received news of the Mahdi's movements along
the White Nile.

Power, an eye-witness to events at Khartoum
in the latter part of 1883, telegraphed a message
to Sir Evelyn Baring, describing the situation.
It gave a vivid image of conditions in a city under
imminent siege, separated by vast distances from
its nearest sources of aid:

> ...At present we are not strong enough to
> seize the well-known ringleaders or agents
> of the Mahdi.   This is well-known to the
> Government, yet over forty days have elapsed
> since it heard the news of our situation here,
> and there are as yet no signs of a relieving
> column arriving. We have not yet even heard
> if they have arrived at Assiout, eight hours
> from Cairo.   On the 27th of last month
> (November) the Khedive telegraphed most
> distinctly that Zubeir Pasha and his Bedouins
> had left Cairo two days before. He said that
> Baker was leaving Suez, yet find that the
> papers of the 4th instant state that neither one
> nor the other have left Cairo, and that Zubeir
> was, before leaving, to raise, arm, and I
> suppose, train 1,000 Negroes. In three days
> this town may be in the hands of the rebels,
> yet there has been an attempt made to prevent
> the Kawah and Duem garrisons from joining
> us.   If Khartoum falls, all Lower Egypt goes,
> as the Mahdi avows his intention of sweeping

across the Suez Canal into Arabia. If Khartoum
falls, every man from here to Assiout will be
in arms to join him as he passes. In Khartoum
many most respectable men who would wish
to be loyal to the Khedive believe him to be
a true prophet. [37]

Desperate as the situation was for Gordon in
1884, Khartoum was still able to muster a strong
defensive force. According to figures compiled
by Moorehead, Gordon had with him in Khartoum
about 34,000 people, 8,000 of whom were soldiers.
Armament included small arms, rifles, twelve
pieces of artillery, and nine armed paddle-boats
that were able to keep up a running fight along
the river. Two million rounds of ammunition
had been stored in the town before it was cut off
and, in addition, the arsenal was capable of
producing another 40,000 rounds every week. [38]
The geographical position of Khartoum favored
the defensive except for its exposed southern
flank fronting on the desert. In the north, it was
protected by the Blue Nile, to the west, by the
White Nile which was more than half a mile in
width. By keeping to the middle of the river,
the paddle-boats could harass the enemy forces
on the banks, at the same time keeping out of
range of the Arab riflemen. Gordon fortified
these zones, but directed his greatest attention
to the south. As Moorehead says:

The weak point in the defense was, of course,
in the south where the town was exposed to
the open desert, but here a deep semi-

circular trench, four miles long, had been dug
from the White Nile to the Blue. From the
first, Gordon concentrated his attention upon
this southern flank. Primitive land-mines
were sown in the sand, along with thousands
of crows' feet and broken bottles—the Arabs
had bare feet and dyed cotton was used to
imitate earthworks while new trenches and
fortifications were being constructed further
back. [39]

By January, 1885, the Mahdi had gathered his
vast tribal armies and prepared to hurl them at
Khartoum. He left the attack to his trusted
Emirs who carried the offensive so aggressively
and so fiercely that the first ramparts were
literally swept away. In the south, the Emir,
Wad el-Nejumi led a powerful force of Ansar
against Khartoum's exposed flank. Within hours,
the city was a sea of Mahdists. Gordon, himself,
met death courageously, brought down by enemy
bullets as he descended the steps of the palace
at Khartoum. [40]

On the eve of the fall of Khartoum the Mahdi
sent the following communiqué to the British and
Egyptian strongholds still remaining in the Sudan:

In the name of God the Merciful, the Compassionate. Praise be to the Bountiful Sovereign, and blessings be upon our Lord
Mohammed and on his family. From the
servant who stands in the need of God, and on
whom he places dependence, Mohammed the
Mahdi, son of Abdullah, to the British and

Shagiyah officers, and their followers: God
direct them to the truth. Surrender and you
will be spared. Do not disobey, else you will
rue it.   And I will briefly inform you, per-
chance God Almighty may put you upon the
path of the righteous. Know thou that the city
of Khartoum and its surroundings are like
the garrison of a stronghold; God has destroyed
it and other places by our hands; nothing can
withstand His power and might; and by the
bounty of God all has come into our hands.

...As you have become a small remnant, like
a leaflet, within our grasp, two alternatives
are offered to you. If you surrender and
prevent the shedding of your blood and the
blood of God's creatures who are under your
leadership, well and good: grace and security
from God and His Prophet and security from
us will be upon you. But if you do not believe
what we have said, and desire to ascertain
the truth of the killing of Gordon, send a
special envoy on your part to see the truth of
what we say: and to your envoy is given the
security of God and His Prophet, till he comes
to us and sees and returns under a guard
from us, to see and to be warned of God. [41]

Moorehead compares the siege of Khartoum
to a Shakespearean drama. He eloquently draws
analogies between the three protagonists: Gordon,
the Mahdi, and Lord Wolseley with the Shakespearean figures of Hamlet and King Lear.
Moorehead says:

There is a fated quality about the events of
the next six months (after August), an air of
pure and certain tragedy that lifts the story
out of time and space so that it becomes part
of a permanent tradition of human courage and
human helplessness.   It can be repeated just
as a Shakespearean tragedy can be repeated,
and it never alters.   The values remain the
same in every age, and the principal characters
are instantly recognizable; we would no more
think of their playing different roles from the
ones they actually played than we would dream
of withholding death from King Lear or of
rescuing Hamlet from his hesitations. Each
of the three main protagonists—Wolseley,
coming up the Nile with his soldiers, Gordon,
waiting and watching on the Palace roof in
Khartoum, and the Mahdi with his warriors,
encamped in the desert outside the town—
behaves precisely as he is destined to do, and
it is wonderfully dramatic that these three men,
who were so perfectly incapable of understand-
ing one another, should have been thrust
together in such desperate circumstances and
in such an outlandish corner of the world.
Each man is the victim of forces which are
stronger than himself.   The Mahdi, having
raised a Holy War, is bound to assault
Khartoum.   Gordon, having committed his
word to the people in the town, is bound to
remain there to the end.   And Wolseley, the
soldier, having received his orders is bound
to try and rescue him.   None of these three
really controls events, none of them can

predict what will happen. From time to time
they feel hope or despair, confidence or
uncertainty, but in the main they simply hold
on to their predestined courses and they are
like the pilots of three ships in a fog that are
headed for an inevitable collision. [42]

The fall of Khartoum marked the zenith of the
Mahdi's glory. The year, 1885, saw a new and
rapidly developing political, military, and religious force in Mahdism. For the next decade and
a half, after the death of the Mahdi, the Central
Sudan would be governed by his loyal disciple,
the Khalifa.

CHAPTER

5

General Gordon and the Sudan: A Brief Biographical Sketch

I am the chisel which cuts the wood; the Carpenter directs it.

—General Charles George Gordon

The first thing for a captain is to gain
Safe victory; the next to be with honor slain.

— Euripides

CHAPTER

5

General Gordon and the Sudan: A Brief Biographical Sketch

Charles George Gordon was one of those enigmatic historical figures who rise rapidly to political and military distinction and then, pass on, just as rapidly, before their great works are completed. Gordon was, in many ways, like the Greek and Roman heroes of antiquity. Like Alexander, he was an excellent administrator and military leader; he had a magnetic personality that had a strange appeal to friend and foe alike; he was restless, yearning for new frontiers; and, finally, he was a deeply religious man. It seemed almost destined that Gordon should find his calling in a vast desert region called the Anglo-Egyptian Sudan.

Who was Gordon, this man of a hundred legends, whose name brings to mind such other English "greats" as T. E. Lawrence and Winston Churchill? What was Gordon's background?

Gordon was born at Woolwich, England on January 28, 1833, the fourth son of the late Lieutenant-General Henry W. Gordon. He was descended from a family tree of soldiers, one of his ancestors being a direct descendant of the Duke of Cumberland, a distinguished officer in the Canadian War under Wolfe at the battle of the Plains of Abraham. Chaillé-Long wrote of Gordon:

> Few men have lived to be so much written of as Charles George Gordon, C. B. Pietist, missionary, and soldier, he is at all times enveloped as with a mantle with the leaves of his Bible. He is a strange composition of a Cromwell, a Havelock, a Carlyle, and a Livingstone. Had he lived in the time of the great reformer, he would doubtless have played some important role.[1]

Gordon has been called an eccentric Englishman with a flair for the bizarre; others have written of him as a man of undisputed genius coupled with a profound moral and physical courage. All of these descriptions fitted Gordon equally well. He was a complex individual, deeply religious, and motivated by a drive for righteous causes which usually included dangerous assignments. C. Rivers Wilson, in a conversation with Lord Salisbury, said:

> If you want some out-of-the-way piece of work to be done in an unknown and barbarous country, Gordon would be your man.[2]

Gordon's early life and schooling mirrored that of a typical nineteenth century soldier. At nineteen, he entered the Royal Engineers and soon took part in the protracted siege of Sebastopol during the Crimean War. Immediately after the War, he served on a Commission which delimited the Turkish frontier in Bessarabia and the Eastern Mediterranean. From 1860 to 1864, Gordon served in China where his first great opportunity for merit and distinction came in 1863 with the outbreak of a Chinese rebellion. Theobald wrote of this aspect of Gordon's military career:

> ...he led a mixed European and Chinese force in the defense of Shanghai against a Chinese rebellion. Inspiring his men with devotion and his enemies with dread by sheer force of personality, he broke the back of the rebellion in a series of dramatic exploits...he returned to England with titles of Mandarin and Field Marshal, conferred on him by the grateful Chinese Emperor...and...found himself a legendary hero with the British public who, henceforward, called him by the affectionate nickname of 'Chinese Gordon!'[3]

Gordon was appointed Governor-General of the Equatorial Provinces of the Sudan in 1874 by the Viceroy of Egypt, suceeding Sir Samuel Baker. On February 20th, 1874, Colonel Chaillé-Long received a note from Gordon requesting Long to join him in Central Africa. The message was short and simple, characteristic of Gordon:

> My Dear Chaillé-Long: Will you go with me to Central Africa? Come to see me at once.[4]

Gordon outlined Chaillé-Long's tasks in the Sudan:

> The Khedive spoke to me about you today.
> You speak Arabic and French. I make you
> chief of staff; you shall command the entire
> Soudanieh army. I don't want the bother of
> soldiers; this must be your work. You shall
> have the rank of Pasha...[5]

Chaillé-Long agreed to go with Gordon but he had trepidations. In his book, The Three Prophets [6] he said that he knew nothing of Gordon until that day when Gordon had requested his services. As Chaillé-Long said: "I knew nothing of the man whom destiny had decreed should be my chief in the wilds of unknown Africa." [7]

Within the next decade, all of England would acclaim the name of Gordon while the inhabitants of the Sudan would view it with awe. When he assumed power in the Provinces, Gordon immediately set out to destroy the slave trade that was flourishing in Central Kordofan, Darfur, and the Bahr el-Ghazal. By 1878, Gordon had begun setting elaborate plans for the destruction of slave caravans. Having reorganized the administration of the city of Khartoum on the White Nile, he felt free to attack the slavers. In 1877, a Slave Trade Convention had been signed between Egypt and England condemning slavery and making the selling of slaves a capital offense. [8] Gordon used all the authority this agreement gave him to thwart the slave-dealers. According to Allen, he wrote in July of 1878:

> We have taken twelve caravans of slaves in two months, which is not bad; and I hope to stop this work 'ere long. [9]

A week later, he wrote:

> I am striking deadly blows against the slave-trade, and am establishing a sort of Government of Terror about it.[10]

The Bahr el-Ghazal was the center of the slave trade and it was, therefore, here that Gordon met his first element of resistance. Suleiman, son of Zubeir Pasha, organized a large force in the province and called for the expulsion of Anglo-Egyptian authority from the slave-caravan routes to and from Equatorial Africa. Zubeir was called to task and asked to explain his son's actions; allegations were made that he had instilled the idea of rebellion in his son's mind. Zubeir vehemently denied these allegations, saying that it was a terrible mistake. His son's loyalty to the government was unquestioned, he protested. When Gordon's representative, Romolo Gessi, killed Suleiman on the grounds of leading a purported revolt, his father brought the case to high officials at Cairo before whom he presented his argument:

> ...About my son, this is what happened: Jealous intrigues at Cairo had poisoned the

ear of the Khedive against me, and I was summoned to the capital. Conscious of no wrong, I came at once, leaving my family and my property in full confidence. Here I found Gordon...I protested my innocence... I offered to go with him and prove...the falseness of the accusations made against me. He refused...told me to write to my son Suleiman ordering him to submit to Gordon.[11]

Zubeir then went on to say that his son gathered twelve hundred followers and set out for Dara where, he believed, Gordon was staying and hoping, in this way, to prove his loyalty. Enroute he met Gessi who ordered him to submit immediately. His son protested and was shot.

The validity of Zubeir's statement was questionable as it involved a personal issue, the guilt or innocence of his son. Gordon pressed the issue to its ultimate conclusion at a special conference held at the British Agency in Cairo on January 26, 1884. Present at the conference were Sir Evelyn Baring, General Gordon, Nubar Pasha, Sir E. Wood, Colonel Stewart, Colonel Watson, Giegier Pasha, and Zubeir Pasha. Gordon invited Zubeir to make any complaints he wished in the presence of Sir Evelyn Baring and Nubar Pasha. The recording secretary wrote down the following dialogue:

Zubeir Pasha: I want to know why my property in the Sudan was confiscated?

Gordon: Because you wrote a letter to your son, Suleiman, inciting him to revolt.

Zubeir: Produce the letter, and then I will speak.

Gordon: It was produced at the court-martial. The Khedive has the letter...Ask the Khedive, your master, for it. I had fifty copies of the trial printed giving the whole history, and containing that letter!

Zubeir: Why did you print it?

Gordon: Because I wanted to show the peoples of the Sudan that I was fighting not about the Slave Trade, but against rebels, and to settle who was to govern the Sudan.[12]

From 1884 to 1885 Gordon established permanent residence at Khartoum. It was in this city that he was to meet the largest onslaught of Dervishes in 1885. Gordon was well aware of the growing power of the Mahdi. Still, he could not believe that these Sudanese tribes, armed with crude weapons, could be capable of launching such heavy and determined offensives.

Meanwhile, in Cairo, the main topic of debate was whether or not to abandon the Sudan to the Dervishes. Gordon had told the syndicate for the protection of the commercial interests of the Sudan: "I do not think that you will ask me to reconquer the Sudan to give it to those who lost it."[13]

In Kordofan, the Mahdi was moving at the head of a sea of Islamic zealots. On the road to Khartoum he dispatched a final ultimatum to Gordon:

You say you have come to make peace because you are with God. We are with God. If you are with God, you are with us; on the contrary, if you are against us, you are against God. Be converted, then, and become a Moslem; if not, we will inflict upon you the same punishment we have accorded to Hicks Pasha.[14]

Chaillé-Long quoted Gordon on his attitudes toward and estimation of the Mahdi's power among the tribes. Gordon's statement revealed an underestimation of the force and momentum of Mahdism:

I am convinced that it is an entire mistake to regard the Mahdi as in any sense a religious leader—he personifies popular discontent. All the Sudanese are potential Mahdis, just as all the Egyptians are potential Arabis. The movement is not religious, but an outbreak of despair.[15]

Such a gross statement reveals the state of mind of a military leader. If Gordon felt so confident about stemming the Mahdist tide in early 1884, the events toward the end of that year must have changed his mind. After ten months of siege the great city of Khartoum fell to the Mahdi's hordes. A defending force of 8,000 Egyptian troops armed with rifles, machine guns, and artillery, and supplied by an ammunition dump which included two million rounds of heavy-caliber bullets was not enough to halt the relentless advance of the 40,000 Moslems who had gathered around the outer ramparts of the city. As resistance in the city collapsed, the surging waves of Mahdists pressed forward.[16]

Finally, Charles George Gordon, himself, fell. He was cut down as he descended the steps of the Palace at Khartoum. With his death, the Mahdi achieved the height of his glory.

In England, bitter clouds of despair hung over the House of Commons. Why hadn't Wolseley arrived in time with the relief column, the public asked bitterly. The British press began running long biographical articles on the now renowned Gordon, comparing him to other great historical figures. A feeling of vengeance and shame arose among the British public; the cry went up to redress this insult to British arms and courage. It was not until 1898 that England recouped her losses in the Sudan, under the iron hand of General Sir Herbert Kitchener.

For Gordon, history had bequeathed a significant niche. The best memorial to his courage and character was written in his own hand:

I declare solemnly that I would give my life willingly to save the sufferings of these people.[17]

EPILOGUE

Epilogue

The Mahdi Rebellion, though it manifested itself in a religious movement, had other, more deeper causes. Holt has broken them down into four principal causes:

(1) The violence which accompanied the original conquest and in particular characterized the Defterdar's [1] devastation of Shendi created a desire for revenge.

(2) The unaccustomed and inequitable taxation, levied by force and augmented by the illicit demands of the officials at all levels.

(3) The attempts of the government to suppress the slave trade which struck at an important source of wealth and the basis of the domestic and agrarian economy of the country.

(4) The partiality shown by the government to the Shaiquiya tribe and the Khatmiya sect, which aroused the jealousy of the other social and religious groups. [2]

To these can be added the expectation of a deliverer (El Mahdi), and the widespread successes of the early tribal uprisings of 1881. It should be noted that the Rebellion did not exhibit the same fervor or enthusiasm throughout its

[1] The Defterdar devastated large regions of the Sudan, including the area of Shendi in an attempt to quell the rebellion of 1823.

[2] Holt, P., The Mahdist State in the Sudan 1881-1898 (Oxford, 1958), page 24.

course. It gained in momentum as the Mahdi gained victories. The most significant actions were, of course, the fall of El Obeid and Khartoum. From 1885, therefore, the Mahdist movement took on more distinct political and military overtones.

The view of the average Englishman in 1899 was more practical. He believed, firstly, that the Mahdi drove the Egyptians out of the Sudan through the better fighting ability of his followers; second, that the Egyptian troops, unassisted by foreigners, could not have defeated the Khalifa; third, that it was England who had reorganized the Khedival army; fourth, British officers led the Egyptian troops and converted them into an effective fighting force which was able to withstand the forces of the Mahdi; fifth, British genius put the finances of Egypt in order and, in this way, enabled the Khedival treasury to finance the major expenses of the Sudan War; lastly, that British units participated actively in the Sudan War and were deemed by the Sirdar to be essential for the success of the Sudan expedition. [3]

These opinions would seem to show that Britain played a dominant role in the Sudan from 1881 to 1898. Indeed, this was true. England's state in Egypt was too great to be lost to an Islamic movement in the Sudan. At the same time, Baring did not want England to assume the economic burden of a protracted desert campaign. He therefore had the finances of Egypt overhauled to accommodate part of the expenses. The tragedy

---

[3] Crabites, P., The Winning of the Sudan (London, 1934), pages 239-240.

of Gordon at Khartoum was due, partly, to the procrastination among the "Consolidationists" at Westminster who wanted to abandon the Sudan entirely rather than finance any more military adventures into this hostile country. They did not realize, in time, that 1884-1885 was a time for decisions. The relief of Khartoum would have meant the re-establishment of a foothold and a bargaining position for England. As it turned out, England was ignominiously ejected from the Sudan and kept out for a period of thirteen years.

Mahdism in the Sudan took a peculiar form. Whereas in other parts of the Middle East, Mahdism was a belief associated with religious redemption and deliverance from evil and poverty and never became a permanent part of the established rites, in the Sudan in 1881, it became not only an active religious force but a political and military one as well. The Mahdi succeeded in molding the Sudanese tribes into a powerful political-military unit through the force of Islam cloaked in the Cromwellian veils of asceticism and renunciation of the material world.

At one point in his career, the Mahdi sought to bring Mohammed al-Mahdi al-Sanusi, the head of the Sanusi order in Algeria into his fold. He offered al-Mahdi al-Sanusi, who bore his own name,[4] one of the four khalifates in the emerging Mahdist state. Mohammed al-Mahdi al-Sanusi was a strong leader among the Sanusi sect not only because of his prestigious family line but

[4] The Moslem World, volume XXXVI, Number 1 (January, 1946) Article: The Sanusis by Charles Adams, pages 25-26.

because of the expectations associated by the masses of his followers with the idea of the "Mahdi" or "Hidden Imam." Mohammed Ahmed saw an opportunity to win over this large and powerful sect in North Africa to his cause. Unfortunately, the Sanusi leader declined the appointment. The Sanusis and the Wahhabis were among the largest and [5] most powerful of the North African sects; had they attached themselves to Mohammed Ahmed and his cause, the British would have faced a most formidable combination. The key factor that lent credence to a possible alliance with the Mahdi was the fact that both the Sanusis and Wahhabis believed in the necessity of a return to primitive Islam. Both believed in the Six Books of Traditions, especially those of Bukhair and Muslim. With minor differences, both sects sought Mohammedan expression [6] with little accoutrements.

Despite lack of support from these sects, the Mahdi went on to carve a large political-military state in the Central Sudan. Hence, Mahdism as a religious force achieved active and energetic propagation, even to the point of military action, in only one area in the Middle East, the Sudan of Mohammed Ahmed.

[5] Ibid., page 26.

[6] Ibid., pages 43-44.

NOTES

Notes To Chapter 1

1. James, F. L., The Wild Tribes of the Sudan (New York, 1893). This book gives a first-hand account of the role that geographical and cultural influences played on the wild tribes of the Sudan during the Mahdist period. James relates his own personal experiences with these Sudanese tribes, organizing and integrating his material into a fine, comprehensive geographical-cultural synthesis.

2. Ibid., pages 1-2.

3. Ibid., page 12.

4. Ibid., page 17.

5. The term, jihad means 'Holy War!' It is an expression of militant Islam, signifying the spread of the Prophet's word by the sword.

6. Abbas, M., The Sudan Question (London, 1953), pages 12-13.

7. Ibid., pages 13-14.

8. Hussein, T., The Future of Culture in Egypt (Arabic) (Cairo, 1938), pages 12-46. Dr. Hussein's book is used liberally by Mekki Abbas to illustrate points of difference between the tribes of the Sudan and between the Egyptians of the Mediterranean coast and the Sudanese of the central regions of the Sudan.

9. Abbas, M., op. cit., pages 13-14.

10. Taylor, A. J. P., The Struggle for Mastery in Europe, 1848-1918 (Oxford, 1954), pages 286-287.

11. Ibid., page 287.

12. James, F. L., op. cit., page 59.

13. The Gambetta Note was the first formal written notice to the Egyptian government by the powers of England and France notifying it of their firm resolve to maintain the powers of the Khedive.

14. Sartorius, E., Three Months in the Sudan (London, 1885) Sartorius' book was published in that fateful year which saw the fall of Khartoum and the rising star of the Mahdi. Sartorius gives her first impressions of the country and its people in a moving narrative.

15. Ibid., page 44.

16.The Mahdi's 'Ansar' were his loyal followers. They pledged themselves to pursue the jihad and to obey the commands of the Mahdi implicitly.

17.Sartorius, E., op. cit., page 47.

18.Chaillé-Long, C., The Three Prophets: 'Chinese' Gordon, Mohammed Ahmed (El Mahdi), Arabi Pasha (New York, 1886)

19.Ibid., iv.

Notes To Chapter 2

1.Chaillé-Long, C., The Three Prophets (New York, 1886), page 72.

2.On November 4th, 1876, Mr. Vivian, Consul-General of England, discovered a deficit of four million pounds.

3.Chaillé-Long, op. cit., page 72.

4.Ibid., pages 74-75.

5.Scott, J. and Baltzly, A., Readings in European History Since 1814: Extracts from the Report of Mr. Cave on the Financial Condition of Egypt (New York, 1930), pages 462-463.

6.Ibid., page 463.

7.Wingate, R., Wingate of the Sudan: The Life and Times of General Sir Reginald Wingate (London, 1955).

8.Ibid., page 15.

9.Ibid.

10.Ibid., page 17.

11.The largest merchant banking houses included Fruhling, Goschen, and the renowned House of Rothschild.

12.Wingate described the methods used to meet the deficits in the Egyptian revenue in his book, Wingate of the Sudan, pages 17-18. Said Wingate: '...to put it another way, revenue was continually being spent in advance, and these advances had to be negotiated in the market. The abracadabra and mumbo-jumbo of banking and even of state treasury practice were freely used about these loans, and words like funding, floating, sinking, and hypothecation star the page. These have some relevance in England, where the system of Dutch finance so acidly described by Canning was and is prevalent, but as applied to the moneys raised by the Khedive of Egypt they merely confuse a simple situation. Egypt or the Khedive had no credit as a western state has; its only credit was a guess that there might be a cash surplus of revenue over expenditure, and this revenue was derived from the land, customs dues, and certain services controlled by the state, such as railways. The development of Egypt would normally have been financed by borrowings—that is to say—private finance would have advanced moneys on terms which a secure system of public finance and administration and the intimate links between the state treasury and private finance, as in the case of England, would have guaranteed. But Egypt was not England or France, and Egypt's security of the state was manifestly less. Therefore, money was advanced by Europe to the Khedive at seven per cent with additional burdens, instead of at two and a half per cent which was the rate of British Consuls; and further, it was secured on theoretically specific assets such as the revenues of a province, which were in fact no security at all as they could not be negotiated though they looked well in the bankers' books. Bad accountancy, extravagance, maladministration, and too fast and too ambitious development resulted in ten years not only in the original loans not being reduced, but in others being added to them, so that by 1876 the Khedive owed ten years' revenue to his foreign creditors and the service of such loans amounted yearly to half a year's revenue. At the same time in England the public debt was some 600 million pounds, revenue was about 90 million pounds, and the service of the debt was 3 million pounds. That is to say the figure of public debt in number of years' revenue was about the same—seven in the case of England, and ten in the case of Egypt but the service in Egypt's case was half the year's revenue and in England's one-thirtieth.'

13. Wingate, op. cit., pages 19-20.
14. Hurewitz, J., Diplomacy in the Near and Middle East, volume I (New York, 1956), pages 191-192. Excerpted from: Great Britain Public Record Office Document, F. O. 78/2997 titled: British Policy on Egypt, October 16, 1879.
15. L. Albertini in his book, The Origins of the War of 1914, volume I (London, 1952), page 29, says: 'From documents and publications which have since come to light

it would seem that as early as 1875 Bismarck, irritated by the coolness of the Italian Government towards an alliance with Germany, favored the view that France should find 'an outlet for her hostile feelings towards Germany' by becoming involved in North Africa...By encouraging Italian ambitions in Tunis, Bismarck would, on the other hand, achieve the object of bringing Italy into permanent conflict with France and tying her to Germany.'

16. Hurewitz, op. cit., page 194.
17. Ibid., pages 195-196.
18. Ibid.
19. The British Ambassador at Istanbul wrote the following message to Foreign Secretary Granville (According to Hurewitz, Diplomacy, page 196): 'The Representatives of Russia, Italy, Austria, and Germany made today at the Porte an identical communication in the form of a pro-memoria in reply to that in which the Porte conveyed to the Governments in question its telegram to London and Paris concerning the identical note to the Khedive.

The communication of the four Powers states that the above Governments desire the preservation of the status quo in Egypt on the basis of the European arrangements and of the Firmans of the Sultan; and that they are of opinion that the status quo could not be modified except by an accord between the Great Powers and the Suzerain Power.'
20. Arabi belonged to that class of Egyptians known as the fellah. This class usually had to struggle very hard to acquire position in Egyptian society. When they did finally achieve distinction, many found themselves still scorned socially by their colleagues. Especially in the Egyptian service was this true. Turkish, Circassian, and foreign officers were treated with greater deference. This situation constituted some of the grievances of the Arabi clique.
21. Chaillé-Long, op. cit., pages 95-97.
22. Ibid., pages 96-97.
23. Ibid., pages 120-121.
24. Ibid., pages 122-123. This communication is quoted from the English 'Blue Book!'
25. Ibid., pages 123-127.
26. Ibid., page 131.

27. Ibid., pages 132-133.
28. Ibid., page 144.
29. Ibid., pages 220-223.
30. Ibid., page 230.
31. Ibid.
32. Ibid., page 152.
33. Ibid.
34. Ibid., pages 152-153.
35. MacMichael, H., The Sudan (London, 1954), page 39.

Notes To Chapter 3

1. The Mahdi's followers were also known as the Ansar. This was a noble term signifying pious and devoted followers with a far-sighted view to the future greatness of Islam.

2. Trimingham, J., Islam in the Sudan (London, 1949).

3. Ibid., page 1.

4. The term, Sudd refers to the enormous swampy area in the clay plain below Nimule. The White Nile enters the Sudan from the mountainous region known as the Bahr el-Jabal, then descends for a hundred miles until it settles as a great marshy area. Up until 1903, the Sudd acted as a barrier to governmental authority in the Bahr el-Ghazal and regions south. By that year, provincial administrations had begun to be set up in these areas.

5. Trimingham, op. cit., pages 2-3.

6. The Moslem World, volume XXXVI, number 3; July, 1946. Article: The Anglo-Egyptian Sudan by Ruth McCreecy, pages 252-253.

7. Ibid., page 254.

8. Ibid., pages 255-256.

9. Trimingham, op. cit., pages 4-5.

10. Ibid. (Special note: Trimingham, J. — pages 4-5.) 'A wide margin of error must be allowed for all official population figures. The earlier ones are mere guesses by Sir R. Wingate and the present day figures are compiled from...rough estimates...Undoubtedly that terrible three-quarters of a century saved the present Government many of the ever-present dangers of over-population. The Government's reluctance to initiate a

103

Census is unfortunate and makes the work of social survey almost an impossibility.'

11. Infra, page 39.
12. Trimingham, op. cit., page 10. Cf. Journal of the Anthropological Institute (1913), xliii, pages 595-610.
13. Ibid., pages 10-11. Cf. Handbook of the Anglo-Egyptian Sudan (1922), page 206.
14. Ibid., page 15.
15. Margoliouth, D., On Mahdis and Mahdiism (London, 1915) Note: Margoliouth's paper is a scholarly and well-documented survey of Mahdism. It offers rare insights into the etymology of 'Mahdi' and 'Mahdism!'
16. Ibid., page 1.
17. Hitti, P., The Near East in History (New York, 1961), page 221. Special note: 'Mu'awiyah, first of the Umayyad rulers, and the real founder of the Arabic Kingdom died in 680 A.D. The succession to his throne was not an orderly one and led to the death of Husayn, the Prophet's grandson, at Moslem hands. Civil war marked the subsequent period.' (Husayn was buried at Karbala which became a shrine second only in importance to Mecca.)
18. Cf. the Works of Ibn Sa'd, volume V, pages 66-86. This can be supplemented by the Chronicle of Tabari, those of Ya'Kubi and Dinawari. Some of this material may be found in the Reference Center of the New York Public Library at 42nd Street.
19. Margoliouth, op. cit., page 2.
20. Ibid., page 9. Taken from Yuwatti'una.
21. Ibid., pages 19-20.
22. Ibid. Taken from Abu Dawud, iv, page 179.
23. Ibid., page 10.
24. The term Dajjal is derived from the Aramaic meshiha-daggala or 'Expected One!'
25. Trimingham, op. cit., pages 148-149.
26. Ibid., page 149.
27. Ibid.
28. Ibid., pages 149-150.
29. Ibid., pages 150-152.
30. Ibid.
31. Holt, P., The Mahdist State in the Sudan, 1881-1898 (Oxford, 1958), pages 44-45.

32. Ibid., page 46.
33. Wingate, F., Ten Years' Captivity in the Mahdi's Camp: from the original manuscripts of Father Joseph Ohrwalder. (London, 1892), page 13.
34. Margoliouth, op. cit., page 20.
35. Holt, op. cit., pages 3-4.
36. The hijra to Jabal Qadir signified another example of the 'flight for the faith!' Cf. sources quoted by Holt in Mahdist State in the Sudan, including Al-Qurtabi (1272) and Tadhkira.
37. Trimingham, op. cit., pages 150-152. From Shouqair, Tarikh as-Sudan, iii, page 123.
38. Ibid., page 152. From Shouqair, iii, page 122. The idea of a Mahdi assumed two main forms among the Sudanese Moslems. Among the Shi'a, the Mahdi was considered as the Hidden Imam who represented infallibility. The other type of Mahdism was called Sunni. It was a popular belief, held in time of crisis, that a 'guided one' would appear on earth to set matters right. As Holt, The Mahdist State in the Sudan, says: (pages 21-22)
'It would perhaps be more correct to call Mahdism a deposit of ideas and hopes rather than an organized and coherent system of beliefs.'
39. The term darawish has been anglicized to dervish. Its meaning is a devout Moslem, poor in earthly gain but strong in religious fervor.
40. Trimingham, op. cit., page 152. From F. R. Wingate, Mahdism and the Egyptian Sudan (London, 1891), pages 47-48.
41. British Sessional Papers: House of Commons, Volume 88, 1884 (Extract).
42. Trimingham, op. cit., page 154. From W. Churchill, The River War (New York, 1899), page 36.
43. British Sessional Papers: House of Commons, Volume 88, 1884. Enclosure 1 in Number 112.
44. Holt, op. cit., page 34. From Manuscript Nujumi-'Abd al-Rahman al-Nujumu.'
45. Ibid.

Notes To Chapter 4

1. Temperley, H., Foundations of British Foreign Policy, 1792-1902 (Cambridge, 1938).
2. Ibid., pages 416-417.
3. Ibid.
4. Ibid.
5. Ibid., page 423. Cf. V. Cecil, Life of Salisbury (London, 1932).
6. Moorehead, A., The White Nile (New York, 1960), pages 180-181.
7. Ibid.
8. Ibid., page 181.
9. Wingate, R., Wingate of the Sudan (London, 1955), pages 95-96.
10. Moorehead, op. cit., page 192.
11. Ibid.
12. Holt, P., Modern History of the Sudan (New York, 1961), page 80.
13. Wingate, F. R., Ten Years' Captivity in the Mahdi's Camp: From the original manuscripts of Father Joseph Ohrwalder (London, 1892).
14. Theobald, A., The Mahdiya (London, 1954), pages 39-40.
15. Supra, page 50.
16. Moorehead, op. cit., page 210.
17. Ibid.
18. Holt, Modern History, op. cit., page 31.
19. Burckhardt, who visited El Damer in 1814, left a description of the Majdhubi theocracy in its last stage. Its ruler, al-faki-al-kabi, 'the great teacher', was Mohammed al-Majdhub (1796-1831), a grandson of the founder. Burckhardt commented on the neatness, regularity, and good condition of El Damer. It became a center for theological studies.
20. Theobald, op. cit., pages 43-44.
21. Ibid., pages 45-47.
22. Among the more renowned of the Emirs was Wad el Nejumi, who led the southern attack force against the city of Khartoum in 1885.

23. British Sessional Papers: House of Commons, volume 88, (1884), Communiqué from Consul Moncrieff to Earl Granville: Number 8.
24. Gordon, J., My Six Years With the Black Watch (Boston, 1929).
25. Ibid., page 111.
26. Ibid., pages 116-119.
27. Ibid.
28. Ibid.
29. Ibid.
30. Theobald, op. cit., page 57.
31. Ibid.
32. Holt, Modern History, op. cit., page 83.
33. A zareba is literally a fence of thorny scrub bushes, extensively used in times of peace to enclose animals, and in war as a stockade. The term was also more loosely used, however, to describe the camps of the slave-traders.
34. Theobald, op. cit., pages 60-62.
35. Ibid.
36. British Sessional Papers: House of Commons, volume 88, (1884) Number 90 (Extract).
37. Ibid., Enclosure in number 194.
38. Moorehead, op. cit., page 234.
39. Ibid.
40. Cf. General Gordon's Khartoum Journal as edited by Lord Elton (London, 1961).
41. Crabites, P., The Winning of the Sudan (London, 1934), pages 4-5.
42. Moorehead, op. cit., pages 237-238.

Notes To Chapter 5

1. Chaillé-Long, C., The Three Prophets (New York, 1886), page 25.
2. Moorehead, A., The White Nile (New York, 1960), page 214.
3. Theobald, A., The Mahdiya (London, 1954), page 18.
4. Chaillé-Long, op. cit., page 27.
5. Ibid., page 28.

6.Chaillé-Long offers significant insights into the character of Gordon in his book, The Three Prophets.

7.Chaillé-Long, op. cit., page 28.

8.The Slave Trade Convention provided for the termination of the sale and purchase of slaves by 1880.

9.Allen, B., Gordon and the Sudan (London, 1935), page 140.

10.Ibid.

11.Chaillé-Long, op. cit., pages 21-24.

12.British Sessional Papers: House of Commons, volume 88, (1884) Enclosure in number 33.

13.Chaillé-Long, op. cit., page 60.

14.Ibid., page 5.

15.Ibid., page 7.

16.See pages 80 - 81.

17.Allen, B., op. cit., page 141.

APPENDIX

Proclamation of Mohammed Ahmed, the "Mahdi"

(Translation)

In the name of God the Compassionate and Merciful, praise be to God our gracious Lord; and prayer and peace upon our Prince Mohammed and his followers!

From the zealous servant of his Lord, Mohammed the Mahdi, son of Abdullah, to his friends in God, to the faithful who believe in God and in His Book.

My beloved, it is known to you all that faith in God and peace with Him is more to man than his own soul and all he possesses, and more than family and brethren, God hath said, 'Family and children will not profit you in the day of resurrection', and as for him whom his relations separate from God, his love cannot last, but the anger of God is upon him, and he will then be anxious to offer up even his parents and belongings as a ransom; but his prayer shall not be heard.

For such men God hath said that they shall be enemies even of their own beloved, but the faithful will not be so; therefore he who believes in God and the Prophet ought to follow the truth and consent to God's judgment, and purify his soul to prepare for the great day. Whoever is longing for bliss ought to ask the same for his own parents and brethren; for every man who is wise knoweth that the day of death is nigh, and the world to come is the world everlasting, wherein we shall behold the Prophet and his followers and our own beloved ones; while the disobedient will be suffering the wrath of God. He is wise who asks salvation for his own soul, not looking back with regret upon earthly ties, but yielding them up for the sake of God. For God hath said in His Book, 'No pity ought to be shown towards your relations and friends when it is a question of setting up the faith, for the love of God.' Love of money and pomp and pride are the first causes of falsehood in the heart of man, and falsehood flourishes therein as plants in streams of water. And they are the faithful who look not to worldly wealth which passeth away from us and must be left behind, for the faithful know their future; and the liars also are aware of their fate.

...The Government now is just as it was in the days of the Prophet, and our times are as those of the Prophet, etc.

21 Regeb, 1301 (May 17, 1884)

(Taken from: British Sessional Papers: House of Commons, volume 88, (1884-1885) Enclosure 1 in number 112.

Unpublished Letter from Gordon to General Stanton

Gondokoro
15th December, 1874

My Dear Stanton,

Those are indeed helps to me, those two officers. They are first-rate fellows, thank you for them. I did not like the phrase of your letter that the Khedive granted the request without 'much hesitation.' Surely he must have seen that I did not want either to increase his expenses or get useless hands. You have but little idea of what work I have up here with one limp, wretched interpreter, Hassan Effendi, who is always sick, an officer in command of troops utterly incompetent, thinking of his own comfort and safety only...I never put a value on myself but I can say that I am worth more than to perish up here with such a set of incompetent apathetic brutes. I do not want you to mention this, for I have written to the Khedive and he has done all I have asked him with great kindness but he has little idea of what I have to go through...I have suffered from liver but it is produced by fieriness and the amount of personal work one has to do. I can quite understand Baker, seeing that his material was rotten, turned his mission into a geographical research, and gave up all idea of a Government, however I have succeeded well enough as yet and have got things into some order and will cover my administration expenses this year and have something over, though it has been at some cost to me

111

personally, for no one could have had a worse set of men with him, than I in my stupidity took. It is only my iron constitution which has pulled me through as yet. Though I say it myself, never will he—the Khedive—find anyone who has stood more, been more insouciant of his comfort or more careful for his—the Khedive's—interests than I have been. He took me of his own accord, I never wanted the Governor-Generalship and in mercy he ought to tell me if I am de trop or not before I die in this land for no purpose. If he is sincere I will go on willingly, if he regrets his bargain, let him tell me so or even hint it to you...Am I a tool to obtain some favor from our Government... etc.

Yours sincerely,
C. G. Gordon

(Taken from: <u>Sudan Notes and Records</u>, volume X (1927) Article: Unpublished letter number 6.)

Gordon's Communication to his Chief of Staff, Chaillé-Long

Gentlemen: As it is well that I should express to you my views before we enter into closer relations, I have thought fit to address you these lines on several subjects:

I. I consider that the provisional form which the expedition has at present will cease after two years' date, and after the lapse of that time it will rest with me to retain or dispense with the services of any or all of the members of the present expedition, as it may seem most conducive to the public service; that is the footing on which I am with respect to the Khedive myself.

II. We are all volunteers, and each one of us is free to come and go from the service as he may think fit.

III. I want from each one of you your best efforts. I want quick execution of orders. I want you not to content yourselves with giving the order, but to see that it is executed, and for you to inform me of its execution. To forget anything comes to the same thing as to refuse to execute it—indeed, is somewhat worse; for in the latter case I can give my orders to another, whereas in the former case I am deluded into a false security and do not take other steps. From my experience, the greatest defects that a man can possess in expeditions like our own are forgetfulness, the not seeing to the execution of an order, being contented at having given it; procrastination and late rising. However talented a man may be, I

113

prefer a stupid man to him if he has the above drawbacks.

IV. My duty toward you is to see that, as far as our means go, you are well cared for; that you are properly supported in your wish; that you have complete control over it, subject to my supervision. With respect to the subordinates you may employ, you will have full power to engage or to discharge, provided that the funds disposable are not exceeded. You shall have all the credit your exertions may merit, and I shall do my utmost to promote your interests.

V. I propose giving each of you so much for servants whom you will select yourselves, my duty ending after I have paid their salaries.

VI. I propose to give you an assortment of the stores which have come from England. This assortment will be for a stated term; if used up before that time, I am not responsible if you suffer.

VII. I will mention that for your comfort it is necessary you have your traveling kit as complete as possible. You ought to pay the greatest attention to this...

VIII. If possible, get on with the Egyptian troops and with the natives. Be loyal toward the Khedive, and consider we cannot weigh the actions of men in these parts in the same scale as we weigh the actions of our people.

Feeling sure that we shall agree with one another, I have the honor to be, gentlemen,

Yours very sincerely,
C. G. Gordon

(Taken from: Chaillé-Long, C., The Three Prophets (New York, 1886), page 35.)

114

Gordon's Letter to the "Herald" Regarding the Cartography of the Equatorial Provinces

Massowa, December 9, 1879

To the Editor: Those who may be interested in geographical discoveries will remember that in 1874 Colonel Long, of the Egyptian staff, passed down the Victoria Nile, from Nyamyonyo, where Speke was stopped, to M'rooli, thus at the risk of his life settling the question, before unsolved, of the identity of the river above Urondogani with that below M'rooli. He also discovered a lake midway between these places, which he called Lake Ibrahim. Passing that way afterward, I ascertained that the native name of the lake was Coje, and wrote this name on the map. I think that you will agree with me that, as maps are made for the use of travelers, the native names should be inserted in preference to names given by explorers, and which are unknown to the native guides.

In writing thus I in no way wished to take from Colonel Long the merit due him for his discovery of this lake, or for his perilous journey.

Those who care to study the successive steps which built up the map of the course of the Nile, will know that to Speke is due the discovery of one portion, to Baker that of another, and to Colonel Long that of another, and of the lake alluded to...

Believe me, yours very truly,
C. G. Gordon

(Taken from: Chaillé-Long, C., The Three Prophets (New York, 1886), pages 46-47.)

115

Burlington Gardens, London,
July 1, 1881

Dear Sir: I am requested by Sir Rutherford Alcock to inform you that he laid your letter to him of the 19th May before the Council of the Society, and they have directed the attention of M. Ravenstein, who is engaged in compiling for the Society a large map of Equatorial Africa, to the matter, with a view to due credit being given to you for priority of discovery and naming of Lake Ibrahim on the map alluded to.

Your obedient servant,
H. W. Bates,
Assistant Secretary

(Taken from: Chaillé-Long, C., The Three Prophets (New York, 1886), page 48.)

116

Consul Moncrieff to Sir E. Malet

Sincat, August 24, 1883

Sir,

I have the honor to detail to you, as I believe, with fair accuracy, the story of the movement in the East Sudan in favor of Mohammed Ahmed, the so-called Mahdi, which formed the subject of my dispatch dated Suakin, the 13th instant.

On the 2nd instant Tewfik Bey, Mohaffiz of Suakin, and responsible for the government of a district which includes Tokar, 14 hours to the south, and Sincat, 11 hours to the west, heard for the first time something of disloyal meetings of Arabs in Erkowiet, a mountainous part lying between the above-mentioned two places at a distance of 10 hours from the latter...Tewfik Bey at once proceeded there and on the 3rd sent to Erkowiet for Osman Digna—said to be the bearer of letters from the Mahdi—and the Cadi of Suakin and an important Suakini called Mohammed Tahir, who were known to be with him. Digna declined to come, but on the forenoon of the 5th appeared together with the above-mentioned, most of the Erkowiet Sheikhs, and a crowd of Arabs which continued to increase from several points until it is said to have numbered at least 3,000. These were armed with big sticks, or clubs, swords, and spears, about half having one or other of the latter. Digna remained at the foot of a hill about 2,000 yards from the barracks, and sent some Suakini Sheikhs and notables to Tewfik Bey with two letters from the Mahdi, addressed respectively to

117

the Mohaffiz of Suakin and the Marmoor of Sincat.
He had also, it appeared, brought a third letter
from the Mahdi to Mohammed-el-Ameen, chief
Sheikh in Erkowiet, which commanded the latter
with much religious fervancy and argument, such
as the assurance of his otherwise certain damna-
tion, to desert the Government and assist his
cause. Mohammed-el-Ameen, however, declined
to be influenced, and though some of his men
joined Digna, and he could not control the other
Erkowiet Shiekhs, as he has usually done, he has
remained, I believe, entirely faithful to the
Government...

...The Mahdi evidently meant to raise this
part of the Sudan to disturb the Berber road and
create a diversion. It is premature to be sure
that he has entirely failed, though I think it merely
rests with the Egyptian Government to secure his
failure. Could Tewfik take Tahir and Digna by
force with or without Arab assistance, the moral
effect would be great...Probably 1 complete
battery of artillery, 2 or 3 mitrailleuses, and 500
infantry, with a man-of-war, the latter with half
the artillery, would, making Suakin and Tokar
secure, if sent at once, meet every requirement.

(Taken from: British Sessional Papers: House of
Commons, volume 88 (1884) Enclosure in number 8.)

Sir E. Baring to Earl Granville

Cairo, November 19, 1883

(Extract)

I Regret to have to inform your Lordship that the present state of affairs in the Sudan is a subject of great anxiety to the Egyptian Government. It is clear that their authority in the Eastern portion of the Sudan is limited to the coast of the Red Sea, and even there it is seriously threatened. As regards the Western Sudan, there has as yet, been no confirmation of the report telegraphed by the French Consular Agent at Khartoum which formed the subject of my telegram of yesterday. But, on the other hand, no definite news has been received from General Hicks since the 27th September. He had only two months' provisions for his army when he started on his present expedition. The Egyptian Government is becoming very anxious and evidently expects to get bad news of him. This morning I saw Giegler Pasha, who was formerly in the Sudan under Colonel Gordon; he says that if General Hicks' army is defeated, Khartoum will probably fall into the hands of the rebels...

(Taken from: British Sessional Papers: House of Commons, volume 88 (1884) Number 90 (Extract).

Mr. Power to Sir Evelyn Baring

Khartoum, December 30, 1883

(Telegraphic)

...At present we are not strong enough to seize the well known ringleaders or agents of the Mahdi. This is well known to the Government, yet over forty days have elapsed since it heard the news of our situation here, and there are as yet no signs of a relieving column arriving. We have not yet even heard if they have arrived at Assiout, eight hours from Cairo...

...If Khartoum falls, all Lower Egypt goes, as the Mahdi avows his intention of sweeping across the Suez Canal into Arabia. If Khartoum falls, every man from here to Assiout will be in arms to join him as he passes. In Khartoum, many most respectable men who would wish to be loyal to the Khedive believe him to be a true prophet.

(Taken from: British Sessional Papers: The House of Commons, volume 88 (1884) Enclosure in number 194.)

Earl Granville to General Gordon

Foreign Office, January 18, 1884

Sir:

HER Majesty's Government are desirous that you should proceed at once to Egypt, to report to them on the military situation in the Sudan, and on the measures which it may be advisable to take for the security of the Egyptian garrisons still holding positions in that country, and for the safety of the European population in Khartoum.

You are also desired to consider and report upon the best mode of effecting the evacuation of the interior of the Sudan, and upon the manner in which the safety and the good administration by the Egyptian Government of the ports on the sea-coast can best be secured.

In connection with this subject, you should pay especial consideration to the question of the steps that may usefully be taken to counteract the stimulus which, it is feared, may possibly be given to the Slave Trade by the present insurrectionary movement and by the withdrawal of the Egyptian authority from the interior.

You will be under the instructions of H.M.'s Agent and Consul General at Cairo, through whom your Reports to H.M. Government should be sent, under flying seal.

You will consider yourself authorized and instructed to perform such other duties as the Egyptian Government may desire to entrust to you.

I am, etc. (Signed) Granville

(Taken from: British Sessional Papers: House of Commons, volume 88 (1884) Number 10.)

His Highness the Khedive to Gordon Pasha

January 26, 1884

(Excellency)

You are aware that the objects of your arrival here and of your mission to the Sudan is to carry into execution the evacuation of those territories, and to withdraw our troops, civil officials, and such of the inhabitants, together with their belongings, as may wish to leave for Egypt. We trust that your Excellency will adopt the most effective measures for the accomplishment of your mission in this respect, and that after completing the evacuation, you will take the necessary steps for establishing an organized Government in the different provinces of the Sudan, for the maintenance of order, and the cessation of all disasters and incitement to revolt.

We have full confidence in your tried abilities and tact, and are convinced that you will accomplish your mission according to our desire.

(Taken from: British Sessional Papers: House of Commons, volume 88 (1884) Enclosure number 3 in number 15.)

<u>Sir E. Baring to E. Granville</u>

Cairo, January 28, 1884

My Lord,

DURING his stay at Cairo, General Gordon intimated to me a wish that an interview should take place between himself and Zubeir Pasha in the presence of Nubar Pasha and myself.

The interview accordingly took place on the 26th instant.

I have the honor to enclose an abridged record of the proceedings. A short-hand writer was present at the interview.

I had a great deal of conversation with General Gordon as to the manner in which Zubeir Pasha should be treated. General Gordon entertains a high opinion of Zubeir Pasha's energy and ability. He possesses great influence in the Sudan, and General Gordon is of opinion that circumstances might arise which would render it desirable that he should be sent back to the Sudan. It would certainly not be desirable to send him there now, for he is manifestly animated by a feeling of deep resentment against General Gordon.

(Taken from: <u>British Sessional Papers</u>: House of Commons, volume 88 (1884) Number 33.)

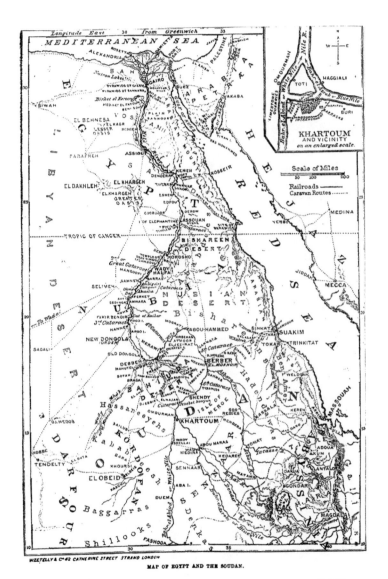

MAP OF EGYPT AND THE SOUDAN.

Taken From: Gordon and the Mahdi: Illustrated narrative (1885)

THE MAHDIST STATE

x   Battle site, with date

- - - - Approximate limit of
Mahdist power at its greatest
extent

RED SEA

Wadi Halfa

DONGOLA

Dongola

Abu Hamad

BERBER

Sinkat   Suakin
Tokar

Berber   SUAKIN
FRONTIER
PROVINCE

Metemma

Karari
1898
Omdurman   x   Khartoum   Kasala
x1885

METROPOLITAN PROVINCES

ABYSSINIAN
FRONTIER
PROVINCE

DARFUR   KORDOFAN

El Fasher

Bara   Dueim
El Obeid   Aba   Sennar   Gallabat
Shaykan   x   Gondar
1883

El Tana

Qadir

Fashoda

BAHR AL-GHAZAL

Daym al-Zubayr

Rejaf

Scale of Miles
0   100   200   300   400

J.V.B.

Adopted from P. Holt,
A Modern History of the Sudan

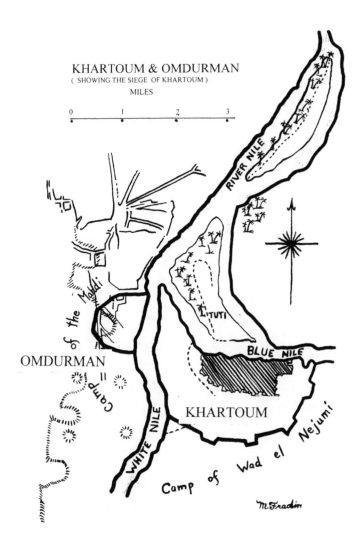

KHARTOUM & OMDURMAN
(SHOWING THE SIEGE OF KHARTOUM)
MILES

OMDURMAN

KHARTOUM

RIVER NILE

BLUE NILE

WHITE NILE

TUTI

Camp of the Mahdi

Camp of Wad el Nejumi

M. Fradin

Bibliography

JIHAD
The Mahdi Rebellion In The Sudan 1881-1885
Bibliography

PRIMARY SOURCES

1. American Oriental Society Journal, volume 31 (New Haven, 1911) Article: A Letter from the Mahdi Mohammed Ahmed to General Gordon.
2. British Sessional Papers: House of Commons, volume LXXXVIII, 1884.
3. Butler, W., The Campaign of the Cataracts; being a personal narrative of the great Nile expedition of 1884-1885 (London, 1887)
4. Chaillé-Long Bey, L'Egypte et ses provinces perdues (Paris, 1892)
5. Chaillé-Long, C., The Three Prophets: Chinese Gordon, Mohammed Ahmed (El Mahdi), Arabi Pasha. Events before and after the bombardment of Alexandria (New York, 1886)
6. Darley, H., Slaves and Ivory; A Record of Adventure and Exploration in the Unknown Sudan (London, 1926)
7. Gessi, R., Seven Years in the Sudan (London, 1892)
8. Gordon, C. G., Unpublished letters of Charles George Gordon in Sudan Notes and Records volume 10 (Khartoum, 1927).
9. ------, Colonel Gordon in Central Africa, 1874-1879; from original letters and documents (London, 1881)

10. ------,General Gordon's Last Journal; a facsimile of the last of the six volumes of journals dispatched by General Gordon before the fall of Khartoum (London, 1885)

11. Gordon and the Mahdi: An illustrated narrative of the war in the Sudan (London, 1885)

12. Gordon, J., My Six Years With the Black Watch, 1881-1887; Egyptian campaign, eastern Sudan, Nile expedition, Egyptian frontier field force (Boston, 1929)

13. Grant, J., Cassell's History of the War in the Sudan (London, 1885-1886)

14. James, F., The Wild Tribes of the Sudan (New York, 1893)

15. Kumm, H., From Hausaland to Egypt through the Sudan (London, 1910)

16. MacDonald, A., Too Late for Gordon and Khartoum. The testimony of an independent eye-witness of the heroic efforts for their rescue and relief (London, 1887)

17. Myers, A., Life With the Hamran Arabs (London, 1876)

18. Peel, S., The Binding of the Nile and the New Sudan (London, 1904)

19. Pimblett, W., Story of the Sudan War. From the Rise of the Revolt, July, 1881 to the fall of Khartoum and death of Gordon, January, 1885 (London, 1885)

20. Sartorius, E., Three Months in the Sudan (London, 1885)

21. Slatin, R., Fire and Sword in the Sudan (London, 1896)

22. Wingate, F. R., Ten Years' Captivity in the Mahdi's Camp, 1882-1892: From the original manuscripts of Father Joseph Ohrwalder. (London, 1892)

125

SECONDARY SOURCES

1. Abbas, M., The Sudan Question (London, 1953)
2. Albertini, L., The Origins of the War of 1914, volume 1 (London, 1952)
3. Allen, B., Gordon and the Sudan (London, 1931)
4. Cambridge History of the British Empire, volume III: The Empire-Commonwealth (Cambridge, 1959)
5. Collins, R., The Southern Sudan, 1883-1898 (New Haven, 1962)
6. Coupland, R., The Exploitation of East Africa (London, 1939)
7. Crabites, P., The Winning of the Sudan (London, 1934)
8. Henderson, K., Survey of the Anglo-Egyptian Sudan, 1898-1944 (London, 1946)
9. Hill, R., Bibliography of the Anglo-Egyptian Sudan (London, 1939)
10. Holt, P., The Mahdist State in the Sudan, 1881-1898 (Oxford, 1958)
11. ----, Modern History of the Sudan (New York, 1961)
12. Hurewitz, J., Diplomacy in the Near and Middle East: A Documentary Record: 1535-1914 (New York, 1956)
13. Jackson, H., The Fighting Sudanese (London, 1954)
14. MacMichael, H., The Sudan (London, 1954)
15. Margoliouth, D., On Mahdis and Mahdiism: from Proceedings of the British Academy, volume VII (London, 1915)
16. Moorehead, A., The White Nile (New York, 1960)

126

17. The Moslem World, volume XXXVI, Number 1, January, 1946. Article: The Sanusis by Charles Adams.

18. ------------------, volume XXXVI, Number 3, July, 1946. Article: The Anglo-Egyptian Sudan by Ruth McCreecy.

19. Paul, A., A History of the Beja Tribes of the Sudan (Cambridge, 1954)

20. Shibeika, M., British Policy in the Sudan, 1882-1902 (New York, 1952)

21. Temperley, H., Foundations of British Foreign Policy, 1792-1902 (Cambridge, 1938)

22. Theobald, A., The Mahdiya (London, 1954)

23. Trimingham, J., Islam in the Sudan (London, 1949)

24. Wingate, R., Wingate of the Sudan: The Life and Times of General Sir Reginald Wingate (London, 1955)

INDEX

Index of Persons

Subject Index

About the Author

Murray S. Fradin holds both Bachelors and Masters degrees in history with a specialization in Middle Eastern Studies. A former history instructor, he is the recipient of numerous honors and awards in his field.

Mr. Fradin has drawn upon his research to bring out a new edition of Jihad: The Mahdi Rebellion in the Sudan. In it he hopes to show uncanny parallels between this century-old war and today's Middle East crisis. He currently resides in New York City with his wife and son where he continues to write.

0-595-27881-7

5709767R0

Made in the USA
Lexington, KY
08 June 2010